30 Nov 2022

To BRIAN —

To a fellow sales man
extraordinaire! I appreciate
the deep experience & Knowledge
you have as well as your
passion for making an impact
in the Global South.

Please enjoy the read + share
with others —

Matt

D1743166

PRAISE FOR
SELL WELL, DO GOOD

"This book demonstrates how the decision intelligence approach transforms selling systems. Roy and Scott capture how each sale has a critical role in behavior change in customers. Working with them to train our sales team has truly been a game-changer for our organization, helping us scale our reach and impact. I recommend this book for inspiration and sales skill-building!"

David Auerbach
Co-founder, Sanergy

"It's clear Roy and Scott have poured a lifetime of experience and passion into their craft of selling. By distilling their expertise and clever, accessible models into these pages, they have created the go-to handbook for anyone serious about selling more to create social impact at scale."

Dan Berlowitz
Founder and CEO, Spring Impact

"A sales team is often the greatest brand touchpoint for a social enterprise. So *how* you sell can build or erode a brand just as much as *what* you sell. DQ Selling is remarkable in that organizations can improve a customer's life—by guiding their knowledge and confidence—without even making a deal. That's critical behavior change. This book shows that entrepreneurs can ditch the old-school, top-down sales approaches and, instead, use proximity and empathy to drive income and impact."

Kevin Brown
Co-founder and CEO, Mighty Ally

"Even the best product won't sell itself. A sales system needs to be purposefully built and a sales force needs to be purposefully cultivated. This is something very few social entrepreneurs know how to do, which is why this book just might be the new social enterprise bible. It is full of practical (and surprisingly simple) tools to transform the way you sell and achieve the impact you want to have. The book guides you on how to start small, but once you start down the path of DQ selling you won't want to turn back."

Emma Collenbrander
Head of Global Distributors Collective

"Having helped thousands of social enterprises grow over the past decade, we have discovered that the two most important ingredients are helping entrepreneurs adaptatively plan as their business grows and improving their sales. Roy and Scott's inspiring, lucid, and practical book will help any social enterprise plan and execute a compelling, adaptable sales strategy that aligns with their values and drives their ambitions to scale to social and environmental purpose."

Nicholas Colloff
Executive Director, Argidius Foundation

"This is the book I wish I'd had when we were on the front lines seeking answers to our questions about how to sell in Indonesia. It isn't hyperbole to say that these authors are among the best in the world at this. My only wish is that this roadmap to crack open sales had been in my hands years ago."

Matt Dalio
Founder, Endless

"This book is a generous gift to social entrepreneurs working across the globe. Through first-hand stories, Roy and Scott inspire readers to toss aside conventional sales approaches that frustrate customers and sales teams alike. They provide practical tools that raise the decision intelligence of their customers and unleash the brilliance of social entrepreneurs and their team members to deliver greater impact. Armed with the right attitude and the collective wisdom in this book, you can't help but succeed."

Lizz Ellis
CEO, International Development Enterprises (iDE)

"Having strong conviction myself that impact investment and social enterprise must be core to successful and sustainable international development, I thoroughly enjoyed the conceptual frameworks and anecdotes laid out in this book. It reflects the authors' wisdom and commitment to teaching effective selling to companies who do good when they sell well. Selling, so they say, is about showing the value of what is on offer. No need for the hard sell with this insightful read!"

Peter George
Senior Advisor, Private Sector & Investment,
Clean Cooking Alliance

"This book will move you from a "job" to a sense of purpose. In my world, we speak of vocation; that is, a job with a higher calling behind it. Learning to sell a valued product with a valued team through meaningful practices will enhance the lives of yourself, your clients, and your colleagues. And your sales will rise in the process!"

The Rt. Rev. Mary Gray-Reeves
Bishop, Episcopal Church

"The DQ framework has been transformational in my own approach to sales and is a critical part of the toolkit I use to mentor and teach. Ultimately, the process of selling comes down to people and their ability to joyfully do their work. The beauty of this book is that it skillfully puts the DQ framework in the context of an organization's people, providing excellent guidance on how a leader can supercharge their team's sales performance."

Laura Hattendorf
Lecturer in Management,
Stanford Graduate School of Business

"A great seller talks little and listens a lot. This is what Roy and Scott model—that sales is not a push, but helping a customer to solve a real-world problem. This book shows not only how to be a great listener, but how to apply this with a formulaic approach across your whole team to achieve your goals."

Ben Jeffreys
CEO, ATEC

"You will fly through this book, its theory explained through deceptively simple, easy to read stories that will challenge your thinking and behavior. Passionate in their conviction that social enterprises must sell well in order to do good, Roy and Scott outline how selling is more about listening than talking. This book draws upon their deep experience coaching social enterprises to sell well and in line with their values—including supporting many Ashden Award winners to greater success and impact in changing the world."

Harriet Lamb
Executive Director, Ashden Foundation

"The social enterprise movement is heralding a business renaissance and Western corporate leaders are taking notice. Many are wondering how to take part in this opportunity and be regarded as valid contributors while maintaining profitability. Roy and Scott, seasoned business consultants to social enterprises for more than a decade, share their invaluable knowledge of how to build and manage sales effectively at the place where money and mission meet."

Howard Lewis
Founder/CEO/Chairman (ret), Family Heritage Life Insurance

"There is no magic bullet for activating a languishing sales organization beset by stagnant or declining sales, embedded attitudes, and the resulting inertia those two key dynamics create. This book provides a pathway to solve that dilemma. It is a straightforward, common sense approach coupled with tools to rekindle sales growth that works with both nascent and established sales organizations. An easy read, packed with solid ideas and uncomplicated methodology."

Ken Lewis
Executive Director, Greater Impact Foundation

"A must-read and share for Social Entrepreneurs across the world. Roy and Scott have created a breakthrough 'step-by-step' formula to do good in a sustainable way for all parties involved."

Stephan M. Mardyks
CEO, Wisdom Destinations and SMCOVEY

"This is a compelling and easy-to-read guide to having impact through sales. With clear frameworks and examples that make it easy to relate to, it offers a step-by-step guide to transforming sales organizations into success stories, salespeople into trusted client advisors, and managers into true coaches. A must read for those who want to make their sales team productive and proud of their job!"

Lucie Klarsfeld McGrath
Partner and Lead of Marketing and LMD Practice, Hystra

"Of all the successful social enterprises I've interviewed on my podcast, many have one thing in common—they've transformed their sales through the DQ Selling process. Roy and Scott have graciously shared their entire process in this timeless book. It is a must read for any social sector leader who wants a practical book on how to do sales right."

Andy Narracott
Host, Finding Impact podcast

"Because people are what make an organization, they are also what can transform it. This is especially important for social enterprises, where creating the conditions for changing the behaviors of both sellers and buyers is integral to the business goal. This book offers a convincing framework for leading and managing B2C sales in a way that is both transformative and impactful. It will be especially of interest to executives with big hearts, who do not like to compromise and who aspire to engineer sales to magnify their impact in the world."

Stefano Olmeti, Ph.D.
Global Executive Leadership coach and Former Head
of Executive Coaching at The World Bank

"I would thoroughly recommend this book for anyone who wants to optimize their sales. The power of the authors' advice is derived first from a deep understanding of people and what drives them. It describes how a better awareness of self and a more enquiring approach to the customer can transform performance. This book also shows how sustainable results come through a gradual and structured improvement process, rather than quick fixes. The authors wrap the theory around a rich collection of human stories, making the book highly readable."

Sam Parker
CEO, Shell Foundation

"This book is designed for innovators who seek to do good in the world and measure their success in terms of impact. Alas, anyone who has ever tried to do good will have discovered that even the best products and services do not sell themselves, and yet it is sales that delivers results. In an easy-to-understand format, using numerous concrete examples, the authors ensure you will no longer mistake sales for an ugly duckling, but recognize it as the noble swan it can become for you, paving the way for your aspiration to make the world a better place for all."

Prof. Dr. Thomas Reuter
Board and Executive member,
World Academy of Arts and Science (WAAS)

"Often people think that selling is a black box, that either you are born with this gift or you will never be able to make it. Well, they are wrong! The book is a delightful journey on transformative selling. Roy and Scott provide a powerful set of tools that lead to ethical selling, with clear benefits for all involved. It is for those who are looking for world-class results based on solid principles that can be learned. You can do good by selling well."

Dr. Patricia Rossi
Asst. Prof. of Marketing, IÉSEG School of Management

"For any purpose-driven entrepreneur who wants to align the impact they make with the money that flows through the business, this book is a must read. The authors elegantly explain why selling isn't slimy and how to do it in a way that feels ethical and scalable."

Dr. Carlos Saba
Co-founder, The Happy Start-up School

"Roy and Scott's techniques have been instrumental in pivoting our organization from a tech-centric start-up, pushing an innovation sold to beta clients, to a fast developing, last mile distributor selling a stabilized offer through a network of agents. I'm glad to see these fundamental frameworks now accessible to social entrepreneurs."

Thomas Samuel
CEO, Moon Senegal

"The DQ Sales® approach is as much a way of life as it is an effective way to transform people, management, behavior, and sales to achieve greater social impact, no matter what you are selling. You will learn a key ingredient to how the development sector must evolve to get sustainable and larger impact. This is a must-read for social enterprises, businesses, and organizations working on strengthening market systems and achieving development outcomes."

John Sauer
Senior Technical WASH Advisor, Population
Services International (PSI)

"Any company that is serious about reaching profitability and creating a lasting impact, must make a deliberate effort to develop their sales teams. Like no other company in the world, WRP has created a toolbox for building sales teams that perform, both in Western and emerging markets. The practice of CLEAR conversations alone has helped our sales team enormously in their work: within a few months a mindset of confusion and anxiety transformed into one of curiosity, discipline and confidence, leading to better sales and happier customers."

Boldewijn Sloet
CEO, SolarNow, Enterprise & Venture Investor

"We learned the hard way that if you can't sell, you can't save the world. "Selling" is not only selling high-impact products; it's also fundraising, persuading policymakers, recruiting talent, and enabling behavior change. Roy and Scott are the go-to black-belts of selling-for-good, and they have been hugely valuable to our Mulago Fellows and portfolio teams. This book gets into the gritty details of doing it well: it's not about the idea of selling, it's about getting good at it so you can make good things happen."

Kevin Starr
CEO, Mulago Foundation

"This is a must-have handbook for every social entrepreneur looking to make a profitable and sustainable impact! With relatable stories and actionable steps, Roy and Scott beautifully outline why it's important to master the art of selling and offer a transformational formula for achieving this."

Fred Swaniker
Founder, African Leadership Group

"Since meeting Scott Roy in 2010, I have seen the Whitten & Roy DQ Sales® approach in action in over 30 high-impact social enterprises across the developing world. I have no hesitation in saying that their DQ® approach—outlined in detail in this book—has been critical in shaping these enterprises into the leading sector examples they are today. In the world of sales, whatever Whitten & Roy put their hands to turns to gold. This book explains how you can capture a piece of that magic to achieve impact at scale. A must read!"

Hazel Taylor
Director, CDC Group

"Roy and Scott explore how to apply human-centered design to sales and ensure social enterprises can scale and thrive. A book filled with relevant case studies and helpful tools and frameworks, I'd recommend it to anyone looking to launch, scale, or lead a social venture of any type."

Jocelyn Wyatt
CEO, IDEO.org

"The COVID pandemic significantly slowed the development of social entrepreneurship. Today's main challenge is how to build back better and multiply the personnel potential. This book is a unique guide not only for new social entrepreneurs but also for those with great experience, because it shows how to apply socially oriented thinking to use selling for doing good and changing behaviors."

Olga Zubkova
Director General of the International Centre for Social
Innovations "Vector of Friendship" Organization with
Special Consultative Status to the United Nations
Economic and Social Council (ECOSOC)

SELL WELL DO GOOD

DQ Selling for
Social Enterprises

SELL WELL DO GOOD

DQ Selling for Social Enterprises

ROY WHITTEN AND SCOTT ROY

Niche Pressworks
INDIANAPOLIS, IN

SELL WELL, DO GOOD

ISBN: 978-1-952654-24-4 eBook
ISBN: 978-1-952654-23-7 Paperback
ISBN: 978-1-952654-25-1 Hardback

Library of Congress Control Number: 2021900924

Published by Niche Pressworks: NichePressworks.com

DEDICATION

To our social enterprise clients whose vision, collaboration, and commitment is an ongoing inspiration.

To the thousands of social entrepreneurs who see opportunities to use business for good and measure profit in terms of meaning and impact as well as money. May this book support you to embrace sales as the noble profession it can be and use it well to do good.

To our dedicated consulting team who have put their talent to work on the wise and noble task of addressing poverty with business interventions, often living in countries far from home and accepting lesser compensation for the rich rewards of having an impact.

TABLE OF CONTENTS

PREFACE

Sell Well, Do Good is written for people throughout the world who are engaged in building social enterprises: the entrepreneurs, their sales teams, and the network of donors, foundations, investors, and accelerators that help them succeed. Every day, thousands of these businesses step up to the challenge of getting their poverty-relieving and life-saving products into the hands of people who need them.

In this book, we apply DQ Selling to the business-to-consumer (B2C) direct selling that many social enterprises employ in emerging markets. It is a companion to our first book, *Decision Intelligence Selling*, which focuses on business-to-business (B2B) selling. Social entrepreneurs may find both books helpful, as they are also engaged in B2B selling activity every time they seek funding, advocate their cause to government entities, enroll partners, or wholesale their products to other businesses.

You may not be familiar with the term "DQ." Just as IQ refers to Intellectual Intelligence, and EQ refers to Emotional Intelligence, DQ refers to the Decision Intelligence of a customer. As Chapter 4 explains in detail, raising a customer's DQ is the path to ethical and effective selling.

While it wasn't possible to interview the hundreds of clients and consultants we've worked with over the past 12 years, we did interview a representative sample. We are grateful for the generosity of their time and their permission to use their names, mention their organizations, and list their websites.

Lastly, we want to acknowledge the significant challenges that the COVID pandemic has brought to social enterprises. Many have had to react quickly, innovate, and pivot to remote selling while learning how to manage their salespeople in creative, new ways. And most are concluding that, when the pandemic is finally over, many of the changes they have made will continue to be part of how they do business. For further ideas on how to adapt to remote selling and management, please consult the COVID resources material in the Books section of our website (WRPartnership.com).

Roy Whitten and Scott Roy

PART ONE

TRANSFORMATION, NOT IMPROVEMENT

CHAPTER 1

SELLING WELL TO DO GOOD

"I've got twenty-three field agents going farm-to-farm selling seeds and irrigation equipment, but it's not working well enough." Mike Roberts leaned forward in his chair.

"We're trying to help farmers earn more, so they don't have to leave their homes for months at a time to work in garment factories or construction sites in the city in order to have enough food, health care, and education for their kids. They can do that by adding vegetables to the rice they already produce."

He touched thumb to fingers, itemizing his points as he spoke. "We've put a lot of effort into the human-centered design process, listening carefully to our customers. We've developed a bundle of farm inputs that will boost production by fifty percent. We've got a simple drip irrigation system to bring water to the fields. The products pay for themselves in less than six months.

But the farmers just aren't buying. We're missing something—I just don't know what it is."

Mike was speaking with Scott Roy, who had come to the two-story villa that Mike's organization, International Development Enterprises (iDE), had converted into its Phnom Penh headquarters. Scott had been in Cambodia for a few weeks, assigned by Voluntary Service Overseas (VSO) to lend his expertise to their Livelihoods program. He had heard about iDE's work in rural economic development and had set up this introductory meeting. The "brief" conversation became a two-hour discussion about Mike's agricultural business and Scott's history as co-founder of a highly successful insurance company that sold its policies door-to-door. At one point, Mike said to Scott, "What you did with your sales organization sounds very similar to what we are trying to do here. We're working to recruit and support a dispersed network of sales agents who are the company's main touchpoints with customers. They need to succeed at selling, or our business fails. And, right now, they're not succeeding."

> "I've always considered sales a black box, a mysterious skill that some people have, and others don't."

Mike took a breath before he continued. "I'm an engineer, not a salesman," he said. "Frankly, I've always considered sales a *black box*—a mysterious skill that some people have and others don't." He thought about his sales staff. "They're isolated out there. We haven't given them much in the way of direction or support. They work on commission, and I know most of them don't earn enough to meet their needs.

"I want to learn more about how you built your sales team. I need a better approach. Something that connects with the customer in a deep, persuasive way. But, for our salespeople, it needs to be *practical*: something they can learn and do. And our managers have to learn how to fix things when problems arise."

He paused, then concluded his thought: "We need *human-centered sales* for our *human-centered products.*"

By this point in his life, being "human-centered" had become part of Mike's DNA. "I was an idealistic young man," he told us later. "I knew that my Canadian middle-class upbringing and education were privileges that came to me by luck. I was looking for ways to give back by helping others who had not been as lucky. My rather romantic notion of giving back included working overseas and doing something useful."

Mike had concentrated his engineering studies on water resources, sensing that knowledge about clean water and irrigation would come in handy. It took some time for him to find the opportunity he was seeking. After university, he got a job with an engineering firm in his hometown of Calgary. It took a few years, but he finally secured a volunteer placement in Cambodia, working as an irrigation engineer.

"Engineering focuses on technical factors," Mike explained, "but I quickly learned that a successful solution also has to consider human factors. You can't just design an irrigation system to fit the physical topography. It also has to work within the social terrain and the local market landscape. Parachuting in and dropping off a piece of technology to solve a problem just doesn't work. You have to involve the *people* who will be using it."

Mike spent three years helping farm communities work together to design, build, and maintain small dams and irrigation canals. Toward the end of his volunteer assignment, he met two people from iDE who were selling foot-powered treadle pumps to farmers in Vietnam and were looking to expand their work into Cambodia.

"Their approach intrigued me," said Mike. "They had a technology that could work at the *household* level. And they didn't approach it as a public works project. Instead, they supported small enterprises to manufacture and sell the pumps directly to farmers. I saw that if you could set up a system to deliver a valuable solution house-by-house, you'd eliminate the need to organize whole communities and avoid a lot of transaction costs. This idea had *legs!*"

Now, he had a business concept that could turn his idealism into a practical solution. Mike kept pondering this idea as he and his new wife left Cambodia to attend graduate school in the States. He spent a year at Cornell University doing coursework, focusing on agricultural engineering with a specialization in water resources. His thesis topic focused on the use of groundwater for irrigation, applying this approach to the physical, social, and economic environment in Cambodia.

As is often the case for social entrepreneurs, one opportunity led to another. Mike returned to Cambodia to complete the research for his degree. While there, he reconnected with iDE, and they contracted him to conduct a midterm evaluation of their treadle pump project, which by that time had been running for a year and a half. "The information they needed for their evaluation was virtually identical to the information I needed for my thesis," explained Mike. That contract ended up funding most of his graduate research costs.

When he returned home, iDE hired him as its first Canadian employee. "I was the Executive Director of a one-person office," he laughed. "I helped donor money find the right projects in emerging markets." As part of his work, he traveled to rural China with Paul Polak, the visionary founder of iDE.

"Paul had incredible energy and an inquiring mind," Mike said. "It was an education to watch how he interacted with farmers. Thirty years my senior, he would rush from place to place and then slow down to spend time listening to a group of farmers. He'd ask dozens of questions to identify the linchpin problems they faced. Then he'd set about matching problems with potential solutions, running calculations in his head to check if they were technically sound and financially feasible. He learned something new from every conversation, and the farmers respected his advice. Years later, when I became the Country Director for iDE in Cambodia, I knew what I wanted to do. I wanted to develop an army of 'mini-Paul Polaks' to help farmers earn more money from their crops."

Now, after several years of effort, he had seen some successes, but not the breakthrough he was hoping for. While talking with Scott, however, Mike saw what he needed to do. He had to crack open that mysterious black box and *learn how to sell*.

"We've been taking for granted that the selling conversation would just take care of itself."

"We've been taking for granted that the selling conversation would just take care of itself," Mike said to Scott. "We've put all of our attention and energy into designing, producing, and marketing our products. We thought that if they were good enough, affordable enough, and visible enough, then all we had to do was send salespeople out to reap a harvest of sales." He gave a shrug and a half-smile. "It's pretty clear that just telling people to 'get out there and sell' isn't enough."

He showed Scott the value chain diagram he had been using to map out his business model. It was a carefully drawn flow chart of boxes, connected by arrows, that tracked how his products flowed from supplier to distributor to field agents to farmers—and how the farmers' produce moved through a network of collectors, wholesalers, and retailers to reach the end consumer.

"I'm now realizing," he said, "that every arrow on the diagram involves some sort of *sales interaction* between the people in the boxes. I've been solving problems within the *boxes*. Now it's time to improve the *arrows!*"

He pointed to the arrow that connected the field agents to the farmers. "It's right *here* that the business sinks or floats. If this sales conversation fails, the value of the entire chain is lost to that farmer and her family."

Mike looked directly at Scott. "Can you *engineer* selling? Systematize it, measure it, boil it down to a process that can be trained and replicated?"

Scott smiled and replied: "Not only can you engineer selling, but you can do it in a way so that, every evening, your field agents will say to themselves, 'I'm proud of what I did today.'"

Mike let that sink in. He extended his hand and said, "That's *exactly* the attitude I want to instill in my organization."

Over the next two years, Mike put this vision into action. First, he worked with Scott to develop a selling strategy for Lors Thmey, which means "new growth" in Khmer and is the name Mike chose for his agricultural social enterprise. They called the field agents *Farm Business Advisors* (FBAs), and they developed a management structure and training program for the FBAs and their managers. They ran a pilot program with a solid data collection system, so the managers could see what was working and what wasn't.

There were successes and failures, but Mike didn't give up. Soon after introducing the strategy, the FBAs' average monthly sales doubled; after two years, it doubled again. Lors Thmey was reaching thousands of farmers each year, and the farmers' income was up by 56%. Mike's conviction—that market-based solutions could make a significant dent in poverty—received international validation when Lors Thmey won the inaugural Nestlé Creating Shared Value (CSV) Prize in 2010.

The following year, Mike requested Scott's assistance to introduce a direct selling system to Hydrologic: another iDE social enterprise that sold water filters to rural families. And he requested an innovation.

He said to Scott, "Just having you train sales agents and their managers for a week or two isn't enough to make things stick. If I'm really going to train my people to sell in this new way, I need a 'mini-Scott Roy,' who speaks Khmer and English, and who *lives* in the field with my sales force for several months: coaching them and conducting follow-up training in real time." This insight launched the development of what would become our organization's field coach role and was another example of Mike's engineering brain at work.

And Mike continued to innovate. He hired two young business school graduates, Tamara Baker and Cordell Jacks, to develop another iDE offering to engage local concrete producers to manufacture affordable pit toilets that were then sold to rural households. They used a human-centered design approach to develop the *Easy Latrine*, an attractive and affordable rural sanitation solution. Over 10,000 toilets were sold during an 18-month pilot. Having proved the concept, they were granted scale-up funds by the Bill & Melinda Gates Foundation, The Stone Family Foundation, and the World Bank.

By this time, we had formed our company, Whitten & Roy Partnership (WRP). We helped Mike, Cordell, and Tamara optimize their model, and, over the next three years, they built a sales engine that sold more than 140,000 latrines and turned iDE Cambodia into the premier rural sanitation marketing organization in the world. John Stone, founder and chair of The Stone Family Foundation, noted that this program has been responsible for raising the percentage of latrine coverage in seven of 26 rural Cambodian provinces from 22% to over

75%. In just the last few years, latrine sales have exceeded 340,000, and this has helped hundreds of villages reach ODF (open-defecation-free) status, and it has played a key role in meeting the UN's Sustainable Development Goals (SDG) in Cambodia.[1]

Recently, we reflected with Mike on our work together over the years. As we looked back at the experience of developing sales methodologies and building sales forces to implement them, he said, "The biggest surprise was discovering my preconceptions about selling and how wrong they were. Selling didn't have to be opportunistic or self-serving. Salespeople could take a fundamentally ethical stance and hold their heads high at the end of the day. Our entire approach to selling was consistent with this stance: no lying or exaggeration to make a sale, just honest education for the customer about the problems they had identified, the cost of doing nothing, and the value of what we were offering."

> "The biggest surprise was discovering my preconceptions about selling…it didn't *have* to be opportunistic or self-serving."

He thought a moment longer. "One thing I really credit Scott with is his sensitivity toward compromise and bad practice. When these crept into our selling process, Scott would

---

1   Specifically, advancing the following SDG goals: Goal 1: No Poverty, Goal 3: Good Health and Well-being, and Goal 6: Clean Water and Sanitation.

consistently point us back to the *true north* of fair dealing and mutual benefit between seller and customer."

Mike shared one last insight. "Contrary to what I'd believed for a lifetime, sales is *not* a black box. It's something that engineers like me can understand and analyze. You don't have to rely on *chance* to find salespeople with some sort of magic-selling gene. You can train and manage it like other skills."

Did it all go smoothly? Was it ever a challenge to make it work? "Of course, it wasn't easy," Mike said, "but engineers are prepared for that. Nothing works perfectly—especially when human beings are involved. We had key managers leave, we uncovered instances of fraud that we had to deal with, and at times, the team strayed from best practice. All of these caused disruptions and made us less effective.

"But fixing problems was easier because we had an underlying system. There was no mystery to it. We *knew* what we needed to do, even when we were doing it badly. After each crisis, we were back and growing again—sometimes on our own and other times with help from you."

His advice to fellow social entrepreneurs? "It requires perseverance. You must be prepared for obstacles, for things to take twice as long and cost twice as much as you think they will—and then you have to multiply those amounts a couple more times. That said, if you've got a fresh idea for doing good, and if it creates real value, there *will be* a way to make it work. And professionalizing sales is a great arrow for your quiver. I learned that it's a science; it's based on principles that you can learn, teach to your employees, and enjoy world-class results."

It's been over a decade since Scott first met Mike Roberts. Our work with Mike has given shape and form to our own company and to what we call Decision Intelligence (DQ) Selling. We've conducted over 350 projects in 44 countries for large companies and small, B2B and B2C distribution channels, complex selling as well as transactional, in both the Western world and the world of emerging markets. In all of these settings, we've seen the remarkable benefits of applying transformational learning to the practice of sales. We've learned two fundamental and surprising things.

First, we've learned that the experience of changing the way people think and act is an activity that *transcends* differences in culture, education, and language. Creating the *conditions* for change and developing an *environment* in which change can happen are both processes that remain remarkably the same wherever applied. This is especially true when it comes to selling and managing the people who do it. Whether they are in New York or New Delhi, Silicon Valley or São Paulo, London or Luanda, people have very similar beliefs about what selling is and how you have to behave in order to be successful at it.

Second, we have learned that *transforming* these convictions and developing a sound selling system is an essential skill for social entrepreneurs. The entire purpose of social enterprise is to achieve impact, to create well-being for everyone involved, *and* to remain financially profitable so you can keep it going. When you align the *way* you sell with the mission and values of your enterprise, you change the behavior of everyone involved: buyer *and* seller. Impact follows, and so does profitability.

As Mike Roberts discovered, DQ Selling is both an art and a science. Making it happen is complex, but it isn't complicated. It's not a mystery; the path is logical and straightforward. But, as with all things genuinely transformational, it will challenge and keep challenging everything that has become *business as usual*—the mindset, systems, policies, and behaviors that, sooner or later, constrain every organization.

If, like Mike, you are one of those leaders who is intrigued by these challenges and want to sell well in order to do good, this book is for you.

Let's go to work.

CHAPTER 2

THE MERGER OF MEANING AND MONEY

Executive Summary

Over the last five decades, a new kind of business with a new kind of CEO has developed in ways both organic and eclectic. Social enterprises, large and small, are responding to a market calling for more enlightened operations that support the well-being of everyone involved *in addition* to generating enough profit to be sustainable and provide a fair, long-term return to stakeholders.

Just as they have transformed the design and production of poverty-relieving and lifesaving products and services, social entrepreneurs can transform the way they sell to align this essential business activity with their mission and values. They can do this by applying the insight and practical skills of transformational science.

This requires *two* transformations: transforming the *way* they sell and transforming the *people* who do the selling for them. Both can be accomplished by applying the formula, R=A+C+E™, to create the conditions that require and empower their organization to achieve the impact they seek to create.

A REVOLUTION BELOW THE RADAR

Mike Roberts sensed he was onto something special. He couldn't know, of course, that he was on the leading edge of a slow-growing tidal wave that was still twenty years away from shore. He was part of a revolution in thinking about the power and purpose of business in a world where a great number of people live in poverty. We're not going to recount the history of this revolution; there are a number of books that do that well.[i] We *do* want to share a few insights and conclusions about what this revolution has generated.

Traditionally, the primary purpose of business has been to generate wealth for its shareholders. For a very long time, addressing social well-being was strictly considered the province of private charities and government agencies. Businesses grew by *selling* their products and services, and NGOs and governments grew by *giving away* money and goods that were generated through private donations and public taxes. In the latter part of the twentieth century, however, recession, globalization, and international conflict revealed serious shortcomings in this arrangement.

While the giveaways of relief funding were absolutely necessary for the poorest of the poor—people ravaged by natural catastrophe, displaced by human conflict, or simply left behind as economies grew—this same strategy was proving too expensive and, ultimately, ineffective at providing economic development opportunities for those trapped in systemic poverty. Additionally, the *project approach* that defined most poverty-relief efforts made it difficult, if not impossible, to sustain initiatives when funding had to be renewed every three to five years.[2] Finally, while business had, indeed, created employment and new hope for many throughout the world, it had also, at times, justified despoiling the environment and exploiting certain people and countries in order to generate wealth for others.

These failings did not go unnoticed. Concerned individuals were thinking new thoughts about the relationship between business, government, and private charity. Mike was one of these individuals. He couldn't see twenty years into the future when the Business Roundtable, a gathering of 181 CEOs of America's largest companies, would declare that the *primary* purpose of business was generating well-being instead of short-term

> Concerned individuals were thinking new thoughts about the partnership between business, government, and private charity.

---

2   About this, Mike Roberts told us: "The start-stop nature of projects makes it difficult to build and maintain momentum, and to evolve through trial and error. This is exacerbated by the fact that there is often only a marginal relationship between the success of a project and its likelihood of being extended or scaled with additional funding. It often depends more on the nature of the fund from which the project grant is drawn (time and financial limits, selection process, and flexibility); and there is also the factor of continued alignment with evolving donor priorities; and the perceptiveness, disposition, and incentives of the responsible people within the donor organization."

profit.[3] Nor could he envision that this simple notion would find a home in the minds and hearts of a new generation of CEOs who wear jeans instead of suits, travel in coach instead of first class, and seek impact ahead of money.

That revolutionary idea—that profitability, whether short- or long-term, should no longer be the *primary* purpose of business—generated a flood of questions: What if we used *business* to relieve poverty and save lives? What if we *sell* our products to the poor instead of giving them away? What if we manufacture and distribute products in a way that creates employment for the disenfranchised? What if we provide a modest, long-term return for our investors while using our profit to increase the impact we are having instead of simply generating more wealth for ourselves? What if we grow a social business to stand on its own and be a source of self-reliance, dignity, and hope for the communities in which we exist?

From these transformative questions emerged a network of people and organizations devoted to social enterprise. We divide this network into two groups: the social entrepreneurs who create and lead these organizations and the people who fund and support their work.

THE SOCIAL ENTREPRENEURS

Many of today's social entrepreneurs incubated their dreams in graduate school courses now being offered at major universities.

---

3   See chapter 2 of *Decision Intelligence Selling* for the full story of this remarkable announcement on August 19, 2019. Although causing barely a ripple in the news and little discernable change in business operations, it remains an interesting indicator of changes in the wind.

The original social entrepreneurs, of course, *grew* into the role in ways both eclectic and organic. Here's how one of them got started.

Paul Polak started picking strawberries at age 12.[4] In a few years, he expanded his efforts to grow the fruit commercially. "My two years in the strawberry business gave me a deep appreciation for what it takes to run a small farm and make money doing it," he wrote.[ii] Many years later, after working as a psychiatrist and exploring the linkages between poverty and mental health, he pursued the answers to two questions that had haunted him for years: What makes poor people poor? And what can they do about their poverty?

By following "a process of jumping on opportunities that appeared unexpectedly and then learning from each experience," Paul first applied entrepreneurial solutions to problems encountered by the homeless in Denver, Colorado. This experience led to "interviewing thousands of one-acre farmers from all over the world who survive on less than a dollar a day." In 1982, he founded International Development Enterprises (iDE) to help social entrepreneurs around the world design products that relieve poverty and ill-health, and then run successful businesses to get these products into the hands of people who need them.

Since Scott's first meeting with Mike Roberts in 2007, we have been privileged to work with many of these entrepreneurs whose brilliance, drive, and skill could have brought them fame and fortune in the commercial world. Why did they choose to

---

4   You will remember him from chapter 1. He was a key mentor for Mike Roberts.

use their business acumen for social good? Here is what a few of them told us.

- Anushka Ratnayake is the founder and CEO of myAgro, an organization dedicated to increasing market access for small-scale farmers in East and West Africa. "I'm an immigrant many times over," she said, "and being an immigrant prepares you well for being a social entrepreneur—developing grit above all else. I was going to study law, but I landed in Sri Lanka just after the tsunami had struck…and that changed everything for me."

- Eduardo Bontempo is the co-founder of Geekie, a Brazilian software company that supports schools to optimize education for children. "I was in investment banking for ten years. I made a lot of money, but what really mattered in my life was education. My father was the first in his family to go to university, and he invested everything he had to give us the opportunity to do the same. I want to make education really work for children, and I want to run a great business and provide a place for people to learn how to succeed, help others in a big way, and provide for their families."

- Esther Altorfer is the East Africa managing director for Sistema.bio, a company that sells biodigesters that turn organic farm waste into renewable biogas and organic fertilizer. "I was working in the developing world at age nine," she said with a smile, realizing how incredible it sounded. "I earned double master's degrees, focusing on impact investing. Reading Mohammad Yunus fired up my imagination about what microfinance could do for emerging markets."

- Kola Masha is the founder and managing director of Babban Gona, a Nigerian company whose stated goal is to "make one million smallholder farmers more money by 2025." "I interned with General Electric when I was studying at MIT, and I worked with Abbey Medical before getting my MBA at Harvard. My wife and I both had great educations, and we were working at wonderful jobs. We realized that we wanted to give back now, rather than wait until we had more money."

> "We realized that we wanted to give back now, rather than wait until we had more money."

- Erica Mackey and Beth Szymanski met at Oxford's Saïd Business School's social entrepreneurship program. After creating and working in social enterprises in Tanzania, they returned home to the United States and started their families. When their search for quality daycare facilities ran into difficulties, they created MyVillage, an organization that trains childcare providers to run professional, sustainable businesses.

There are thousands of people like this throughout the world. Their abilities *and* their limitations have led to the development of another group of people who are dedicated to helping these entrepreneurs succeed.

THE PEOPLE WHO SUPPORT THEM

Social entrepreneurs don't make it alone. Many of them are upheld by a loose network of investors, grantors, incubators, accelerators, universities, and consultants in specialized fields. This network has deep roots that merge social and environmental commitment with business rigor.

One example is Santa Clara University's Miller Center, located in the heart of Silicon Valley, who state that their purpose is to "leverage entrepreneurial spirit with the University's Jesuit heritage of service to the poor and protection of the planet."[iii] Lisa Mikkelsen of Flourish Ventures (a spin-out of the Omidyar Network) brings years of corporate HR experience to her role. She helps social entrepreneurs recruit, train, and manage the talent they need to create the impact they desire. John Stone of The Stone Family Foundation, a successful entrepreneur himself, is adamant that social enterprises need "to run as effective, sustainable businesses."

It has become obvious to huge funders, such as USAID, the Bill & Melinda Gates Foundation, and the Shell Foundation, that money alone does not guarantee success for these social enterprises. Many of these organizations now fund specific programs providing technical assistance in key areas. And, increasingly, one of these areas is sales.

Laura Hattendorf is the head of grants and investments at the Mulago Foundation and a lecturer at the Stanford Graduate

School of Business, where she teaches a course for aspiring impact entrepreneurs. She told us, "Sales was never taught as an essential skill when I was in business school. Now, it is firmly on my radar."

Kevin Starr, managing director of the Mulago Foundation and a former ER physician, puts it more bluntly: "It was obvious to me from the beginning that our social entrepreneurs were smart as hell, creative, passionate, and oblivious to the need for selling—and correspondingly *terrible* at doing it."

SELLING IS THE KEY

Some social entrepreneurs start their businesses knowing that selling well is essential to the success of their mission. Eduardo Bontempo brought ten years of investment banking experience to his leadership of Geekie. "When we launched our product in 2017, we saw right away that it was innovative and had a market fit. So, it made sense for us to invest in a sales team. The economics of the business were promising, but we needed a sales approach that aligned with the methodology of our educational product."

Other social entrepreneurs learn an interesting lesson: if you're first to market with a great product, your early success may conceal an inadequate sales strategy and capability. "When you did the discovery process with us in Mexico," said Esther Altorfer of Sistema.bio, "it forced us to look in the mirror about the way we were selling. But we didn't put that learning into practice; we were in the middle of an expansion into Kenya, and we thought we were doing okay because we were succeeding there."

She laughed and shook her head. "In all our years in Mexico, we had only sold 1,000 biodigesters. In our *first* year in Kenya, we sold 1,200! We were like, 'We know how to do this!' However, the following year, a drought hit Kenya, and sales fell well off. We didn't know what to do in hard times."

Learning *how* to sell is a challenge that most social entrepreneurs don't anticipate. Their education, at some of the best universities in the world, focuses on needs analysis, design, manufacturing, finance, and the development of supply and value chains. The closest they get to any formal education on the science and art of sales is usually a class in marketing. As many social entrepreneurs are now realizing, marketing is necessary, but it is *not* a substitute for sales.

Lizz Ellis, CEO of iDE Global, stated it plainly: "If you have goods, services, and products that are meant to create social impact, you won't be able to have that impact unless you have a solid sales strategy that you can execute on."

John Stone also doesn't mince words: "You've got to become profitable enough to be stable and self-sustaining, or you'll forever be dependent on annual renewals of your funding, and you'll fail in your social mission. The key to successful social entrepreneurship is *selling*."

We find that social entrepreneurs routinely make two fundamental mistakes. The first is to think that if you get the product and marketing right, selling will happen on its own. The second is to believe that you can hire sales managers who will know how to set up your selling

> "The key to successful social entrepreneurship is *selling*."

system. Months into setting up their business, social entrepreneurs can wake up to a sales nightmare because they failed to pay as much attention to sales strategy and execution as they did to design, supply chain, and funding.

If you're going to do good, you've got to sell *well*. Not only do you need a selling system that works, you need one that *aligns* with the integrity of your mission. *And* you need to develop a sales force that does their work ethically, proudly, and skillfully—right down to the step-by-step details of how a sales agent empowers customers to think clearly, buy wisely, and commit to new behavior. Nearly always, this requires more than mere improvement; it requires a *transformation*.

TRANSFORMATION IS THE PATH

Recently, the word "transformation" has become popular in business circles. Unfortunately, as popularity rises, the power of a fresh word diminishes with overuse. We knew that the word had eclipsed its expiration date when one of our commercial customers referred to a 30% reduction in sales staff as a "cost transformation." Let's explore for a moment what a transformation *really* means. Then, we can address how it's done.

We first encountered the concept of transformation during the 1960s when it was applied to personal development in what has become known as the Human Potential Movement. It described a radical shift in human thought and behavior—a profound and permanent change from the norm.

In the late 1990s, transformative learning became its own field of study.[iv] Today, it draws on a wide range of thought and practice: from ancient wisdom to modern neuroscience. It focuses on *how* human beings undergo fundamental, permanent change—as individuals, in groups, and in institutions. When applied to the field of sales, it requires addressing both *context* (what people believe about selling) and *content* (how they actually do it). It offers a unique understanding of how social entrepreneurs unconsciously utilize an outdated approach to selling and why that just doesn't work for socially-minded organizations. And, in Mike Roberts' words, it offers a way to "engineer" a selling system that delivers impact year after year.

All of our clients, in both Western and emerging markets, utilize a simple formula—$R=A+C+E^{TM}$—to *create the conditions* in which a transformation in sales can occur (see Figure 2.1).[5] This process requires addressing four fundamental elements to transform selling systems in a way that is simple, practical, and integrated:

---

5   In 1986, Scott attended a training program cofounded by Roy. Afterwards, he created this formula to use in his own business. Now, it is the framework that guides WRP in our customer delivery and the running of our own company.

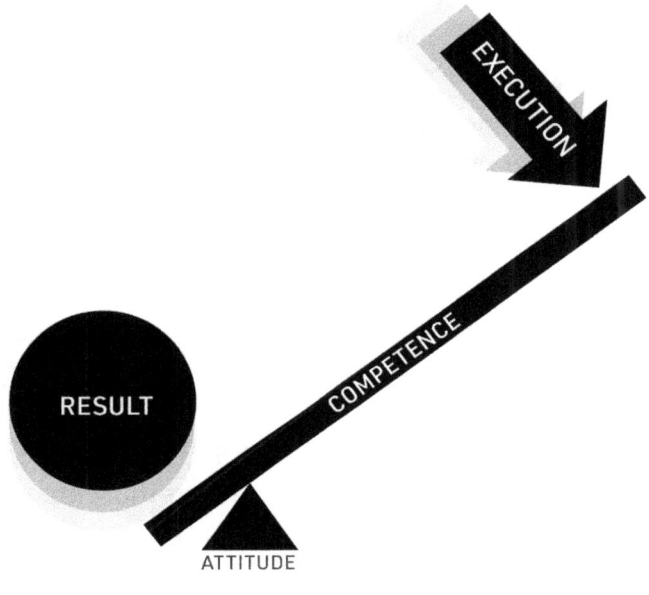

Figure 2.1 R=A+C+E™ – A Transformational Formula

- **Results.** Focusing on the sales results they're seeking and the activities that will create them. Transformation is about *getting results* and getting them in a way that people are proud of and *want* to keep doing.

- **Attitude.** Noticing their state of mind as they work. At any given moment, are they really *committed* to what they're doing, taking full responsibility for their targets, and maintaining a mindset that gives them greater access to their natural brilliance, boldness, and ingenuity?

- **Competence.** Mastering the art of having conversations that move things forward: selling conversations that engage customers, build trust, and generate committed action; and sales management conversations that keep everyone thinking deeply, collaborating fully, and developing their expertise.

- **Execution.** Doing the right thing at the right time with the right people: a sales and management system that actually *develops* the customer's decision intelligence and that the sales force actually *wants* to be a part of.

When you successfully address all four of these elements, you experience two fundamental transformations that empower your sales force to sell in a way that genuinely promotes the well-being of everyone involved *and* increases revenue and profitability.

First, you transform the *way* you sell. The next section of this book (Part Two) walks you through how to do this.

- **Chapter Three** explains the fundamental challenge to be faced: the core convictions about selling and managing salespeople that *everybody knows* are true (spoiler alert: they're not).

- **Chapter Four** introduces Decision Intelligence Selling— a framework that sales teams follow in their door-to-door and group sales conversations to build trust by leading their customers to make the best possible buying decisions.

Second, you transform the *people* who do the selling to free their ability to adopt new practices and keep themselves from defaulting to old behavior when the pressure is on. This is absolutely critical for *any* sales team and especially for the newer teams that often operate in emerging markets.

Part Three of the book shows you how to apply R=A+C+E™ to develop your sales force in this way.

- **Chapter Five** illustrates the very human problem R=A+C+E™ addresses. It describes *autopilot*, a way of living and working that we all fell into around the age of five. And it provides a practical, scientific explanation as to why focusing on the development of new habits is problematic.

- **Chapter Six** focuses on the "R" in the formula, *Results.* It reveals the value of, and the practical steps involved in, cultivating what traditionally has been called *Deep Desire*. It's a way to aim your brain and generate what we refer to as the *natural brilliance that allows people to achieve the results they seek.* We share the neuroscience that explains how we lost the boldness and creativity we had in childhood, which now, as adults, we can recover.

  > The ability to manage your own mindset, moment-by-moment as you work, is an immediate path to peak performance.

- **Chapter Seven** concentrates on the "A," *Attitude.* It introduces Split Attention, a simple technique for immediately moving into present-moment awareness. It's at the heart of all our transformational practices, and it generates the wisdom, the passion, and the courage to make everything else work. This chapter introduces the ability to manage your own mindset moment-by-moment as you work—an immediate path to peak performance.

- **Chapter Eight** addresses "C," *Competence,* by introducing CLEAR™: a way to engage people—customers, colleagues, direct reports—that generates genuine trust, clear understanding, and committed action. Mastering this conversational skill allows sellers to lead customers to a decision and managers to develop the sales capability of their teams.

- **Chapter Nine** unpacks "E," *Execution.* It lays out the steps to implement DQ Selling and achieve the sales results that deliver the social impact you seek. It explains how to design a simple system that eliminates wasted effort and unnecessary distractions for sellers and managers. It illustrates how to create the conditions that require and support your sales force to focus on the right activities, maintain an effective mindset, and *continue* to develop their skills as they work.

- **The last chapter**, Very Next Steps, is exactly what it says. It will get you started without overloading your circuits.

Two Final Comments:

You'll notice the word *we* throughout the book when normally an author would use *I*. We use it because we've written this book the way we developed our business. One of us thinks of something first. We then discuss it in detail, and the end result is a joint creation: something that neither of us could have developed on our own. So, unless it's critical to the story or just too inaccurate to attribute a thought or an action to both of us—for example, Scott's work with Mike Roberts before we started working together—we will be using *we* throughout the book.

Lastly, we want you to know that the stories and comments in the book are real. We interviewed 21 clients, partners, and consultants, all of whom graciously agreed to our using their names and that of their organizations. Occasionally, we create a composite character from the many other clients we've worked with. And, a couple of times, we include comments from people who wish to remain anonymous.

Onward.

PART TWO

TRANSFORMING THE WAY YOU SELL

CHAPTER 3

UNNOTICED BAGGAGE

Executive Summary

You can't change what you can't see. Step one in any transformational process is to **perceive reality accurately**—to observe what your salespeople and sales managers are actually saying and doing. That clear-eyed understanding of what's happening leads you to connect the dots in new ways—to see the system at work, the prison in which you're living.

What does your selling behavior tell you about what your people actually believe selling is about? What are your salespeople actually doing with customers? What are your sales managers actually doing with your sellers? See this clearly, and you'll see what needs to be changed.

"We had been evolving a way to help existing organizations achieve more impact and develop more effective leadership.

Then, we made a big pivot. We thought: 'Let's get promising leaders with a good idea and a start-up organization. Let's get them *early* in their process and help them be deeply intentional about how they are going to fulfill their mission.'"

Kevin Starr paused as he reflected on his early days as managing director of the Mulago Foundation. "We worked with a variety of people, including leaders from big NGOs, agencies, universities, and social entrepreneurs—people who'd started their own organizations to take a good idea to scale. Overwhelmingly, we found that it was the social entrepreneurs who were best able to turn our teaching and money into real impact that could scale."

We asked him, "And how did it happen that you focused on entrepreneurs—both for- and non-profit businesspeople—who wanted to use tools and principles of business to accomplish a specific *good* in the world as opposed to simply generating more wealth?"

"Well," Kevin replied, "we started with an approach to philanthropy that treats impact as the analog of profit. Once we did that, we arrived at our definition of social entrepreneurs: people who have an idea about how to solve a serious problem and want to build an organization to develop that idea, prove it out, and scale it up." His voice raised a bit, and he spoke with more passion. "And many years ago, an important mentor said this very simple thing to me: 'Impact is all about behavior change. If people don't *do* something different, nothing changes.'"

He smiled and continued. "Really, we're just a bunch of money trying to change behavior. We work with our social entrepreneurs to help them take effective action on their own behalf to achieve the impact that they—and we—aspire to. They are really smart people; they make the most of the tools we've developed to help them figure it out."

> "Impact is all about behavior change. If people don't *do* something different, nothing changes."

Let's take a look at what some of these smart people are discovering about what they know, and don't know, about the part selling plays in the impact they long to have.

When social entrepreneurs bring to a country a new product or service that can make a significant difference to many people, they show up with passion, intelligence, and perseverance. Sometimes, however, they don't notice that they have dragged along with them old ideas and practices about sales. This baggage from the past often locks them into behavior they don't know to change until they see that it costs them dearly.

THE PROBLEMS TO SOLVE

"There are so many challenges for these social enterprises to overcome," reported Karen Genzink, a WRP senior consultant who worked for seven years on various projects in Africa, Southeast Asia, and Mexico. "Weather, difficult roads over great distances, village politics—a salesperson can handle all of that, and then, when they approach the house where their customers live, they find that only the grandmother is there, caring for the children. Mothers and fathers, who are often the breadwinners and decision-makers, actually live all week long in the local city where the factories and paying jobs are located. There are *many* hurdles to overcome, and it can be enormously frustrating."

Lizz Ellis highlighted another systemic challenge. "The market for our products gets distorted by well-intentioned subsidies from governments, NGOs, or companies engaged in corporate social responsibility. For example, a provincial government may have provided a financial subsidy for some people to buy a toilet, but that support is limited. The offer expires, and then others in the village refuse to buy a toilet with their own money because they're waiting for the next handout. That wait could be anywhere from one to ten years!"

John Stone expanded on this thought. "There are different *levels* of poor," he says, "and the poorest of the poor *do* require a subsidy for a toilet. But this must be done in a way that doesn't spoil the marketplace, or else the entire village won't become open-defecation free—a tragic and unintended consequence."

Gayatri Datar, co-founder and CEO of EarthEnable, pointed to the necessity of developing quality products. "We had to admit that our first solution to sanitizing dirt floors just wasn't good enough. It's hard to sell what doesn't work. Once we improved the product to have a better market fit, we finally saw our sales fly."

Kola Masha had the opposite problem. "Our services are designed to make small farmers more money. Early on, our services worked so well that our sales agents didn't actually have to spend much time with farmers in order to get a sale. We were not growing as fast as we wanted, however, and we realized we had to make some changes in the way we were selling.

We needed a *structure*, a process for selling that went beyond simply presenting a value proposition. We had to teach our agents to really *listen* to the farmers and *dig* for the problems they were facing."

John Stone highlighted the challenge facing every social enterprise. "They must be run as efficient, effective businesses, complete with a solid selling system. If an organization is first to market in a given area with a reliable new product, it will sell without a lot of effort. Marketing is important, but it's *not* selling. For a company to achieve the long-term sustainability that fulfilling their mission requires, they've got to have a selling system and be disciplined enough to follow it. Nothing else lasts."

Anushka Ratnayake was visiting Proximity Designs in Myanmar when she happened to observe a WRP consultant who was working with the company. "I met this guy who was so young but so good at sales. He actually knew *how* to sell and how to teach others, too. I wanted to get someone like that to help us figure out how to sell our savings program to farmers in West Africa."

Esther Altorfer shared her delight at figuring out her selling system. "Learning that there actually was a consistent way to sell biodigesters was eye-opening for us!" she exclaimed. "We figured out how to sell, and our sales managers learned how to manage. It made *all the difference*."

Chhavi Sharma of Ashden commented on another kind of

> When social entrepreneurs acknowledge that they must become as expert at selling as they are at product innovation, things change.

selling activity that social entrepreneurs encounter.[6] "They often struggle for funding; organizations have to *sell themselves* to people who are looking for places to put their money. And these donors have their own individual reasons for giving. You've got to find out why they give and see if your needs match their reasons. Mostly, social entrepreneurs simply show up and present their case for being funded. That's just not good enough anymore."

When social entrepreneurs acknowledge that they must become as expert at selling as they are at product innovation, things change. Erica Mackey, co-founder and former COO of Off-Grid Electric (now Zola), shared her experience in Tanzania: "When you try to hire local salespeople, you find that either they've never sold before, or they've only sold fast-moving consumer goods. You just can't sell pay-as-you-go solar to individual consumers and small businesses in the same way you sell SIM cards and cigarettes."

Eduardo Bontempo had a similar insight into sales managers. We shared with him our observation that social entrepreneurs often go outside their organization to "find experienced sales managers." He laughed and said, "Well, I've made that mistake. We worked with you to develop a selling system, and we trained our managers to use it. They kept our sales agents on track, and it worked." He paused a moment, as though to emphasize his next point. "And then we launched an expansion

---

6   Ashden is a UK foundation that creates an ecosystem of support for entrepreneurs who focus on climate solutions.

and hired managers from the outside whom we just didn't have the time to train. They brought their own ideas about selling, and now, half of our sales force is working against the other half. I'm going to fix this, and from now on, we won't 'hire' sales managers. Instead, we'll *train* them in the system we have developed."

Lisa Mikkelsen had an insight as to why social entrepreneurs pay so little attention to both the system of selling and the development of the people who run the system. "It's unfortunate," she said, "but many social entrepreneurs think that anyone can sell—that it's just a matter of telling people to get out there and do it. And the same is true of sales managers." She thought a moment and then concluded, "Actually, they just haven't thought about sales in any sort of critical or deep way."

And that is the unnoticed baggage that many social entrepreneurs bring with them to their work. They may have consciously left behind the trappings and purposes of traditional, commercial enterprise, but often they are still hindered by old ways of thinking about selling.

IT AIN'T WHAT YOU DON'T KNOW

*"It ain't what you don't know that gets you into trouble.
It's what you're absolutely sure of that just ain't so."*
—ANONYMOUS, BUT OFTEN ATTRIBUTED TO MARK TWAIN

All of the social entrepreneurs with whom we've worked have sooner or later had to crack open what Mike Roberts called the *black box* of selling: discovering what it actually is and what it takes to make it work. This is the point at which we usually engage social entrepreneurs for the first time: when things are going wrong. Nearly always, their companies are missing their sales targets. Often, they are trying to scale, fend off competition, or increase penetration of their market to achieve the impact they desire. It's challenges like this that reveal the deficiencies in their approach to selling. It's a painful *and* creative space, filled with new possibilities because old practices have failed to produce the desired results.

Poor selling and dysfunctional sales management cost companies time, money, and energy, all of which are already in short supply. When the initial passion for *doing good* starts fading in a sales force, complaints arise about things like unreasonable sales targets, bad territory, unfair compensation, and long hours. Sales curves start to flatten, even decline. Turnover in staff accelerates with missed targets, and performance milestones are missed. Customers start complaining about the way they are being treated—before and after they buy—and the most valuable commodity of all, the company's reputation, begins to suffer.

But here is where social entrepreneurs have an advantage over many of their commercial counterparts. They care deeply about the mission they're on and the impact they want to make. This sense of mission is what has been called *Deep Desire*. This hunger—to do good—is what drives them to shine a light on the critical activity that needs their attention. They start asking two questions: "How *do* we actually sell?" and "What isn't working?"

They bring to their search the same open-mindedness, curiosity, and determination they originally brought to the founding of their enterprise and the innovation of their products and services. Invariably, social entrepreneurs discover that they and their colleagues have been locked into a system of behavior that the science of transformative learning refers to as a *paradigm*—*a* set of processes and practices people default to whenever they think about, plan for, or engage in "selling."

> This hunger—to do good—is what drives social entrepreneurs to shine a light on the critical activity that needs their attention.

Paradigms are surprisingly resistant to change. From *inside* the paradigm, everything makes sense—it feels like you *have to* do things a certain way, even if they don't work particularly well. Furthermore, you can't just *talk* people out of their paradigm. One writer said that getting people to understand the paradigm in which they're stuck is like trying to get them to bite their own faces. Another described it as talking about freedom to prisoners who have forgotten that there's a life outside the prison walls.

The Prison[v]
Picture a prison in which the inmates have been incarcerated for so long, they have completely forgotten that they used to have a life of freedom outside the prison walls. They no longer spend their time remembering how life used to be or planning for life following the completion of their sentences.

Instead, all of their energy and activity is devoted to "getting ahead" within the prison. They compete for upgrades to their cells, awards for being productive prisoners, and recognition for contributions to prison art and literature—all of which support the notion that life in prison is all that exists.

There are therapists to help prisoners adjust to life behind bars, spiritual leaders to help them aspire to be the best prisoners they can be, and elected prison leaders who maintain the social order.

If anyone ever wonders, "Is this all there is?" they are quickly reassured that the answer to that question is, "Yes, this is it."

Transformational science identifies ways to shift established paradigms. First, you have to help people see what they are losing, the price they are paying for continuing to operate as they are. Then, you must help them uncover the *assumptions and convictions* that underlie how they've been behaving. You shine a light on the things that "everyone knows for sure that just ain't so," and then you see who wakes up to what's been happening. Then, if these people can *experience* behaving in a new way—if they can see and hear the benefit of doing so—things can actually change...and quickly.

There is often one central conviction at the heart of every paradigm, something that everyone is so "absolutely sure of" that no one asks if it's really so. Kevin Starr had this figured out from the moment we met him. "Everybody thinks," he said, "that selling is all about *hustling stuff.*"

Brilliant! This ubiquitous belief—that selling is fundamentally pitching and persuading people to buy—drives sales agents to deliver convincing arguments *before* finding out what their potential customers actually want and need. Salespeople talk instead of listening, and they pitch instead of inquiring. And, of course, customers *expect* to be hustled or even lied to. When salespeople come to their doors, they actually *ask* to be pitched: *What are you selling, and how much does it cost?*

Furthermore, this conviction—that selling is persuading people to buy stuff—has a detrimental effect on the entire sales team. Most sellers don't actually *enjoy* doing what it takes to constantly convince and persuade other human beings to buy from them.

And, since hustling isn't inherently satisfying, sales *managers* have to convince their salespeople to *keep* doing what they don't enjoy: pitching, pursuing, and pressuring their customers to buy. How do they do this? By doing their *own* pitching, pursuing, and pressuring using both carrots and sticks to get salespeople to work long hours, hit their targets, and pressure their customers to buy...or else.

When social entrepreneurs see this paradigm at work in their own organization—the organization they built from the ground up, often at a significant personal sacrifice, now struggling to fulfill its mission—they often feel two powerful emotions: *embarrassment* at what they overlooked and *determination* to be as brilliant in their selling as they have been in the development of their products. They're ready to break out of the prison that the old paradigm of selling has kept them in and create something entirely new: a selling system and a way of executing it that aligns with the good they wanted to do in the first place.

Now, they are ready for selling in a way that changes behavior—for the customer, for the salesperson, for the manager—for everyone involved in the sales process.

CHAPTER 4

DQ SELLING

Executive Summary

DQ Selling transforms the transactional sale into a conversation that creates behavior change in your customers.

When you let go of *convincing* customers to buy and replace it with a selling process that *leads* them through a four-step conversation about Problem, Cost, Solution, and Value, you create the conditions in which they can make a *choice* to buy and use your products and services.

Not only does this create impact, it creates pride, competence, and discipline that makes selling fulfilling for everyone involved.

Picture yourself in a training venue—anything from a conference room to a raised platform under a thatched roof.

Welcome to the first morning of your sales transformation program. You've already worked with your consulting team to develop the training that you and your company's sales managers are about to experience. You've also enrolled your leaders from finance, marketing, and operations; you want their work fully aligned with the transformation in the sales process that you are about to implement. You're cautiously optimistic about what's going to happen; you're hopeful but want to remain realistic about the problems to be solved. You lock eyes with Joseph, your COO, who gives a gentle nod. You sense that this could be a pivotal moment in your company's young history. This isn't going to be an overnight fix, but you anticipate a solid launch of a new selling future for your Kenyan enterprise.

> This isn't going to be an overnight fix, but you anticipate a solid launch of a new selling future for your enterprise.

At nine o'clock sharp, you welcome everyone and set the context for the next few days: full participation, best thinking, challenging the status quo, no work interruptions, and, above all, complete honesty. You've had this group of people spending part of the past two weeks observing your sales agents in the field and also watching each other work—all with an eye to discerning *what* the "company" thinks about selling and *how* "we" actually do it. You're looking forward to hearing what this group—the people most committed to the impact you want to achieve—has observed and experienced. You also want to share your own thinking about a pathway for sales that is as brilliant as the products you offer.

The trainer instructs you to find a colleague you're willing to speak with openly and to turn to page three in your workbook. A question is written at the top of the page: "Based on what you observed in the field, what do you *really* want from this training?"

You're given a few minutes of silence to reflect and write. You look at the notes from your own observations. Your team spends way too many hours trying to find the *right* customers, chasing leads, jumping into each other's territories. You know your sales managers are doing most of the selling for the weaker agents, covering for them, and simply failing to develop them into productive salespeople—although, you admit to yourself, you're not exactly sure what "developing" their salespeople might entail. You've heard the rumblings of discontent about favoritism shown by managers who hire family and friends or tribal allies instead of people more qualified to sell. You know that much of the sales data your agents and managers report are either exaggerated or downright falsified. Whenever Gideon, your head of sales, has tried to challenge your sales managers about these issues, he's hit a wall of excuses, reasons, and counter-complaints.

You start to write. Your first few sentences are the normal stuff—you want the sales teams to hit their targets, quit complaining about how hard things are in the field, and stop wasting time. You want them to just *get on with the job:* knocking on as many doors as possible instead of traveling great distances to chase low-hanging fruit and then asking for more travel allowance. You're sympathetic to the challenges they face, but you want them to learn how to do the job well, enjoy it, and be fully committed to what they agreed to do.

You want *all* the people sitting around this table—sales managers and leadership alike—to think more deeply about selling, to stop making the same mistakes over and over, and to learn how to *fix* what isn't working instead of excusing it. You want accurate and timely sales data and forecasting that has a basis in fact. You want a simple, measurable system of selling in which everyone knows their part and just keeps getting better at it over time. You want the entire company aligned with the selling system, using their brainpower to work *with* the process instead of staying in their silos and hoping that sales will somehow magically happen.

The trainer then asks you to share your thinking with the colleague you're sitting with. As you exchange thoughts with your partner, you're surprised at the emotion you feel. You didn't realize how much this has been bothering you. You're actually relieved to be here with your senior team addressing these things. And you're beginning to wonder what everyone else is sharing about *your* leadership of them.

THE WAY IT'S BEEN

After the discussion in pairs, the trainer pulls the group together and asks a surprising question: "How many of you ever sold anything before joining the company?" Three of your four sales managers raise their hands; the other one looks at his workbook as if wanting to find somewhere to hide. No one else on the leadership team has had any direct sales experience. *That's* an eye-opener.

The trainer asks another question: "How many of your *salespeople* have previous sales experience?" The sales managers share what they know about their teams. It turns out that nearly a third of their agents haven't sold anything before joining the company, and a great majority of the rest only had experience selling fast-moving consumer goods. Gideon mutters, "There's a big difference between selling solar and soda."

> "There's a big difference between selling solar and soda."

The trainer lets the comment pass, but the point is made. There's something to learn here. "Would you be willing," the trainer asks, "to adopt a beginner's mind as if you knew nothing about selling?" The group nods their agreement.

"Okay," the trainer says, "now, as objectively as possible, describe what you observed your company's salespeople *actually saying and doing* in the field."

Yaro, the CFO, speaks first, as if stating the plainly obvious: "Every agent had a box of lights. They knocked on doors and demonstrated how the lights work. Customers were generally impressed by the amount of clean white light that was put out. A few people bought right away. Other times, they gave some reason as to why they couldn't sign up, usually financial; at that point, our agents either walked away or kept trying to talk them into buying." He can't resist a final jab. "It's a simple job." You make a note to reexamine the wisdom of having your CFO set the sales targets.

The trainer asks for more detail. Mercy, your marketing director, who conducts the company's sales training, adds, "The agents were doing what I taught them to do. They kept the box of lights closed at first. They started by being friendly—you know, chit-chat to break the ice. Then after a minute or two, they asked if the customer had solar lighting and, if not, they read the value proposition I had printed on the box. Then, they unpacked the box and demonstrated how the lights work."

Gideon adds, "I saw a few agents doing something different. When they opened the box, they handed some of the components to the customer to hold. Then they helped the customer connect the lights to the central battery pack while they explained how the system works. That took about five minutes, and I think it helped the customer see how easy it is to use the system. That was pretty smart."

You notice most of your colleagues' heads are bobbing up and down in agreement. Mercy isn't done yet. "That's okay to do, as long as they've already explained the features and benefits of the system and how payments work," she says, with more than a little emphasis. "That way, customers understand what a good deal it is." She pauses a moment. "Of course, that's when customers would start objecting," she observed, "but if the agent just kept on explaining well enough, sometimes it worked."

As the group shares their observations, it's obvious that agents are doing different things in their efforts to make a sale. It's also obvious that there is one behavior they have in common: they talk a lot more than they listen.

Then Joseph makes a thoughtful contribution. "I spent time watching Akinyi work. I knew she was our best salesperson, and I wanted to see what she did that made her so successful.

One thing I noticed was that she was really good at getting her customers to open up. Much of the time, she actually listened *more* than she talked. Her 'sales pitch' looked more like a conversation between two old friends."

"I think Akinyi is the exception," says Jewel, the HR director. "I saw most agents start out relaxed and polite, but sooner or later, they put on the pressure."

"You should see them during the last week of the month," Jimiyu, a sales manager, said. There was some laughter around the room, but not a lot. He kept talking: "What I mean is, *of course*, they put on the pressure. They've got targets to hit, and they *need* to press, or they're not going to hit them."

"And it's your job to pressure *them* to pressure the customers?" asked Jewel.

"Well, yes," Jimiyu replied. "You've got to stay on top of them to get the job done. I call and text throughout the day to check on them, then I catch them when they come into the office. If I don't, they start sliding. I know this makes them anxious at times, but I don't know what else to do." That comment opens a long discussion about the *pressure* everyone—agents and leaders alike—is feeling.

Then Frank, your most senior manager, who has been with the company from its inception, does something that defies culture and tradition. He looks directly at you and says, "Well, boss, all that pressure starts with you, doesn't it?"

This is hard to hear, and you're wise enough *not* to say what you're thinking. Instead, you swallow your pride and reply, "Can you give me an example?"

Frank thinks a moment, and then he says, "Do you remember when you called me into your office last week and said, 'Here are your new sales targets'?"

"Sure," you respond. "Our lead investor was disappointed that we missed our projections during the first half of the year, so they required us to increase production in the second half to make up for it. So, we had to calculate new targets." You realize that you're now using a lot of words, explaining instead of listening, and you have a sinking feeling that you've missed something important.

Frank lays it out for you. "We already *had* an agreement about targets for the rest of this year, an agreement that you said wouldn't change. Six months ago, I got our entire sales force to sign up for those targets. We've worked hard this year, and now you put even more pressure on us. That doesn't help!" The room is completely silent.

You have a moment of startling clarity. Well, you think, *that* took guts. And trust. That's why you value his opinion, and even more, his willingness to demonstrate to the rest of your leaders that you don't have to keep quiet to keep your job.

Yes, you do remember the conversation. You had reported your results to your board. Your investor had demanded that sales get stronger, your finance director had jumped on board, eager to improve the reporting for the year, and you had simply gone along with it all. You realize now that you had *sensed* there was something wrong with this strategy, but you were preoccupied with the next evolution of your product design and analyzing the possibilities of expansion. You just didn't follow the intuition that has guided you well in the past.

Thoughts follow in rapid succession. Pressure is felt throughout the organization, but it's the sales force that receives the brunt of it. They constantly get pushed to work harder, sell more, and do it all faster; in turn, they push customers to buy. No wonder your salespeople talk more than they listen.

Pressure is felt throughout the organization, but it's the sales force that receives the brunt of it.

You admit that Frank is right, and you acknowledge him for his honesty. That eases the tension in the room, and you sense that it paves the way for more truth to be told. You're glad that, over the years, you've learned to admit your mistakes.

The trainer senses that this is a hot topic, and he gives everyone additional time to identify the pressure points and the breakdowns in your selling system. The group comes up with a long list. You're intrigued by the fact that many of the items are things you could fix without having to consult with your board and funders. That's promising.

Then, over the next hour of conversation, you see something genuinely interesting happen to the group. Somehow, it's become apparent to the group that *everyone*—from senior leadership to sales management—has been believing that selling is *convincing* and, if necessary, *persuading* customers to buy. It is so obvious that it's amazing no one has mentioned it before. It's like the Emperor's New Clothes—everyone sees that the Emperor is naked, but no one says anything. Now, they're speaking up.

You have an insight. It's not that this purpose for selling—*convincing customers to buy*—isn't right. It's that it just isn't right *enough* to fulfill the mission you're on. It reduces the sales conversation to a simple transaction: you give me money, and I give you this product. That sort of exchange moves some products out the door, but not in numbers sufficient to deliver the mission *and* be profitable. The way you've been selling is *transactional*, not transformational.

Furthermore, when it comes to changing a customer's habits and practices, convincing and pressuring is not an invitation that is exactly welcoming. Nor do your sales agents want to do it. No wonder they drag their feet as they approach the next doorway or dial the next phone number.

When the conversation turns to an alternative way of selling that is far more effective at changing behavior, your ears are wide open.

THE WAY IT CAN BE

What if your sales agents weren't trying to *persuade* customers to buy but instead were *increasing their ability to make their best buying decision?*

The trainer introduces a new line of inquiry. "Here's something that may strike you as strange, even impossible. Imagine what it would be like if a sales agent wasn't trying to *persuade* a customer to buy but instead was *sharpening that customer's ability to make the best possible buying decision*—even if that meant the customer *didn't* buy from your agent on that particular day." You can feel resistance to this notion—in yourself and around the room. But you did commit to bringing an open mind, and you join a small group to consider the idea.

The trainer adds a final instruction. "Don't *debate* whether raising your customer's ability to make the best decision is a *better* idea than convincing them to buy. Just concentrate on what it would *be like* for you to sell this way. Be specific. What would you do, and not do, during that conversation? What would you say? What would you not say? How much would you talk? How much would you listen? And—" he paused a moment to capture their attention, "discuss what it would be like *for your customers* to be approached this way. What would be *their* experience if they knew you were helping them make a thoughtful decision instead of just talking them into buying?"

The discussion is eye-opening. What interests you most is how relaxed, enthusiastic, and engaged your entire team has become. And you notice how often they spot a practice, a habit, or a process that would have to change—including in parts of the business that aren't strictly sales. This is intriguing.

The trainer says, "What I'm about to share with you is *more* than your sales agents need to know, and we will talk later about what their training will include. But, as the leaders of this company, *you* need to fully grasp what it means and what it takes to sell in this new way. Once you've got that understanding, you can each bring your creative expertise to align your entire company around it in order to generate the societal impact you wish to achieve."

He stands and turns to a flip chart. He draws the X- and Y-axes of a graph—only the Y-axis points down instead of up, and the numbers 0 and 10 appear at either end of the lines (see Figure 4.1).

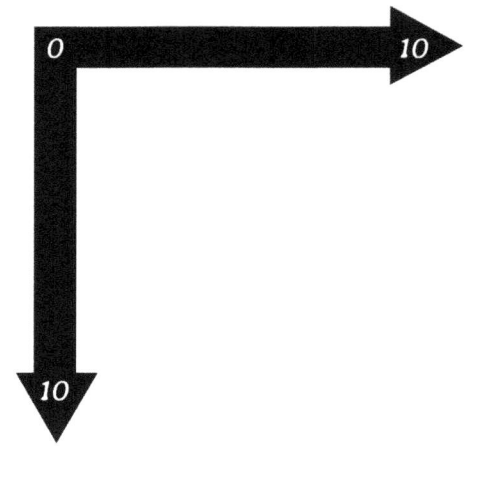

Figure 4.1 Decision Intelligence Selling

Problem

"Now," the trainer says, "let's look at how you would help someone make their best decision about whether or not to buy what you're selling, instead of trying to talk them into it. There are two fundamental things customers must understand if they are to make an informed, intelligent buying decision. What are they?"

Makena raises her hand. "They've got to understand the features and benefits of what we're offering." The trainer lets the answer hang in the air.

Jimiyu breaks the silence. "But before that, they've got to realize they have a *need*."

Jewel, who's never worked in sales, sums it up: "Well, *that* makes sense—the customer has to understand what they need *before* they hear about what we're offering."

"Exactly," says the trainer. And, if customers have a clear understanding of the *problems* they have—a ten on a scale of one to ten—*and* they really grasp how your product or service *solves* those problems—again, an understanding to the maximum level of ten—would it be accurate to say they have 100% of the information they need to make their best buying decision?" (See Figure 4.2.) No one disagrees; they're quiet and thinking deeply.

The trainer continues. "When you sell like this, helping the customer discover the problem *before* you propose the solution, we call it DQ Selling—*DQ* stands for Decision Intelligence. We're suggesting, of course, that raising a customer's DQ is the focus and ultimate purpose of all your sales conversations. You're *not* trying to convince them to buy; you're leading them to make an *informed decision* that will help them and their families." The trainer lets this sink in for a moment and then says, "Of course, this is simple to say and challenging to do."

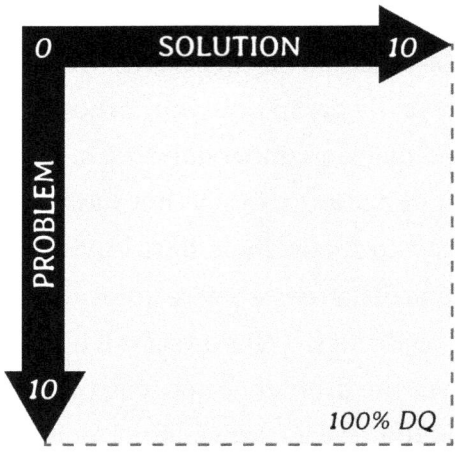

Figure 4.2 Decision Intelligence Selling

This stimulates a few minutes of discussion from the group. DQ is a novel idea. It's logical. It's a strangely attractive concept, but, like others in the group, you have questions about what exactly it would entail.

"Well," the trainer says, "let's look at how to do this. To help customers understand the problems they have to solve, you have to guide them through two specific steps. The first step involves understanding the problems they actually have. The second involves calculating the cost of leaving those problems unsolved." (See Figure 4.3.)

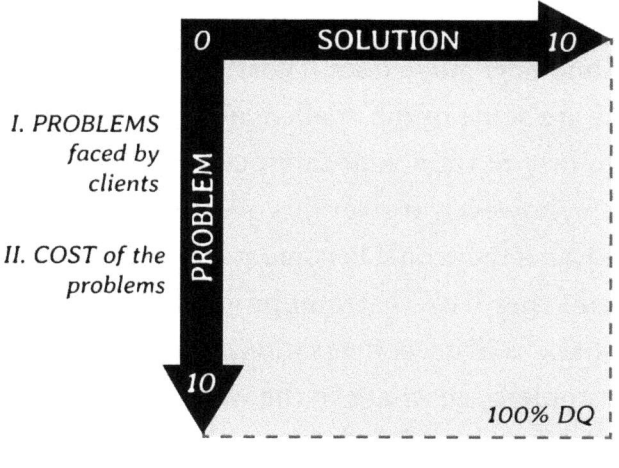

Figure 4.3 Decision Intelligence Selling

He writes the steps on the chart and says, "Let's talk first about helping your customer discover their 'problems:' the specific challenges and issues they are facing that your product could help them with. Then, he asks a direct question: "What might be *preventing* your salespeople from doing this with your customers?"

The group offers some thoughts: "Agents can't take that much time;" "Customers have other problems we can't solve;" "Agents can't change the way they behave;" and "Customers don't actually *know* the problems they've got; they're just used to living with them."

Moses, another sales manager, chimes in. "And what if customers don't *want* to tell us? That happens to my agents. I've been *trying* to get them to ask their customers questions, but they tell me that the customers just keep asking, 'So how does this work…'" he pauses, and several people complete his sentence: "…and how much does it cost?" Everyone laughs.

"Those are some of the challenges," the trainer says, "and we'll get to how to train your salespeople to handle them. For the moment, however, answer this question: What would your customers *gain* if they could become aware of, and acknowledge, the problems they have that your product solves?"

That sparks a lively conversation, summed up by Makena. "When customers see what's in the way, then they can choose to do something about it," she says. "I'd *like* my agents to do that for our customers. It would give customers real reasons to buy what we're selling—*their* reasons, not ours."

Cost

That opens up the subject of Cost. "By *Cost*," the trainer says, "we mean both the money customers are spending because these problems exist *and* the nonfinancial impact of having these problems persist. Can anyone give an example of the price your customers pay by *living* with their problems instead of *solving* them?"

Jewel has something to say. "The solar lighting systems we provide can save families a significant amount of money they currently spend on kerosene and candles. And it provides *safe* light for children to study by after the sun goes down. This prevents a lot of other problems from developing. More money is available for school and growing the family shamba,[7] and who knows where a good education will take the children!"

---

7   In East Africa, a *shamba* is a family farm.

The trainer senses that this example has stirred the group's interest. He puts everyone into small groups again, this time with different team members. Your task is to reflect on your customer conversations and, with the benefit of hindsight, make a list of the problems that customers were actually facing and what it was costing them to leave these problems unsolved. Your group discusses three specific customers. You develop a chart of twelve problems and an estimate of what each problem was costing one or more of the customers.

When you return to the large group, the combined insight of what people share is extraordinary. The list is long and detailed, both quantitative and qualitative. And when calculated over multiple years, the total Cost of the problems is *huge.*

The trainer captures this information on multiple flip chart pages, hangs them around the room, and asks a simple question: "How does this information help your customers make a good decision on whether or not to buy your products?" The group offers several answers: it gives customers a wake-up call about the money they are losing; it generates legitimate concern about their present circumstances; and it creates not just interest in what you're offering but a strong urgency to do something about it.

Frank adds a shrewd observation. "And what's really good about this," he says, "is that if there are no pressing problems to be solved or if the Cost isn't high enough, they have no reason to buy our products." The group laughs hesitantly, and then Moses adds, "But that's a good thing, right? They can say 'No thanks' and know *why* they're saying it. And we can move on to the next house or shop without wasting time trying to talk them into buying." Frank just smiles.

These are intelligent and thoughtful observations. You're beginning to see how this can work. As you look around the room, you can see that you're not alone.

Solution

After a coffee break, the trainer turns to the Solution axis of the graph. "Just as there are two steps required for your customer to fully grasp their problems, there are two steps in helping them understand the solution you are offering." The trainer writes "Solution" and "Value" on the diagram (see Figure 4.4).

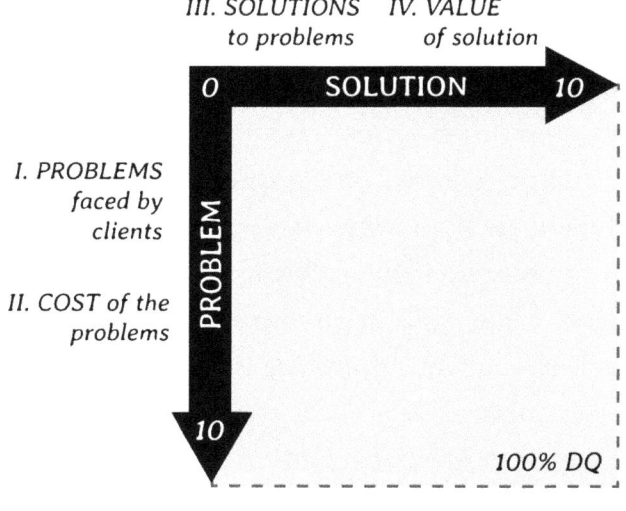

Figure 4.4 Decision Intelligence Selling

Now, you're on more familiar ground. Your agents are pretty good at talking about the solar devices you offer; it's just that they've been doing it too *early* in the sales conversation. The advantage of waiting until customers identify their particular problem is clear. "Now we know what to talk about!" Joy says, as she snaps her fingers. "And we don't have to share *everything* our products do, just the things that actually solve the problems that are costing the customer so much time, money, and concern." You notice that the trainer keeps quiet and lets Joy's words sink in.

Gideon fills the silence: "And we're not really 'pitching' anymore, are we? We're simply showing customers how solar solves their specific problems." He smiles, pauses, and then offers a final thought. "Our agents actually *like* solving problems."

Value

"Okay," the trainer says, "let's return to the sales conversation. You've taken the customer through three steps. Perhaps it's taken ten minutes; perhaps it's taken thirty. It doesn't matter. What matters is to complete the process by helping your customers envision the Value your solution brings to their families."

You sense where the trainer is heading, and you understand the importance of taking the customer through this final step. This is where the customer takes over the conversation, where they imagine a new future for themselves, a future that actually wasn't possible until your sales agent knocked on their door.

The group develops a number of helpful questions to ask the customer at this point: "How much money will you save over the next year? The next three years? How much more can you earn if you had fewer of these problems to handle? What else do you want to do with that time, energy, and money?"

You sense that the discussion has landed on solid ground. Raising the customer's DQ has brought a new possibility into the room, a new way of selling that actually cuts deep enough to *create* the change in behavior that's required to have a lasting impact.

The trainer, however, isn't finished. He has more reality to introduce: "How many of you suspect that when your customers say hello to your agent, they aren't exactly expecting to have this four-point conversation?"

Most of the group raise their hands. Several of them share how cautious and suspicious customers are—how reluctant to share their thoughts with a salesperson at their door.

"Let me show you why they're so hesitant," the trainer offers. He points at the Problem axis. "Think about your most thoughtful customers. On a scale of one to ten, how deep does their understanding go about *all* the problems they are trying to solve *and* the price they're paying by leaving them unsolved?"

The group reflects on the selling conversations their agents have had with customers. How aware *were* the customers of the challenges they faced and what they were costing? They come up with an average rating of 8 for their most insightful customers and 3 for their least informed customers. Then, they score their customers on the solution axis. Their most experienced customers score a 6—they don't know anything yet about the solutions your company may be offering—and the least sophisticated customers score a 3.

The trainer draws some dotted lines on the graph, creating three squares as he plots the responses (see Figure 4.5). Even the most informed customers only have a 48% DQ. The least informed customers have a staggeringly low 9% DQ. When you compare these two percentages with a full DQ of 100%, it's easy to see why customers hesitate to buy and come up with objections.

When customer DQ is low, what you're selling is only a "nice idea" that feels expensive. When their DQ is high, it becomes a "must-have" for which they can find the money.

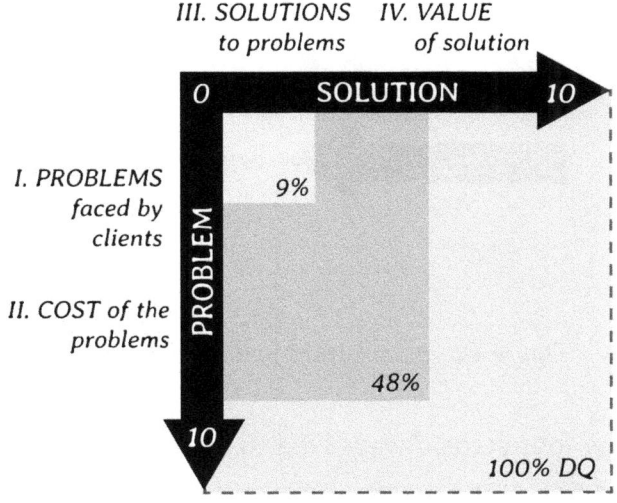

Figure 4.5 Decision Intelligence Selling

The trainer adds four words to the diagram on the flip chart and presents the *experience* a customer has during this four-step journey (see Figure 4.6). As customers gain a deeper awareness of their challenges, they feel more concerned. When they calculate the cost, they feel a sense of urgency. The understanding that there is a solution to meet these challenges brings relief and confidence that they're on the right track. And estimating the value of that solution generates a willingness to pay for it.

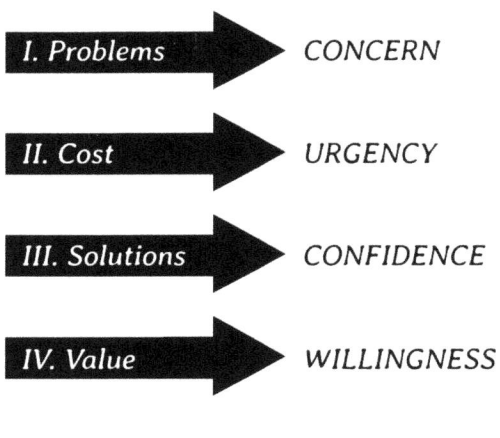

Figure 4.6 Impact of DQ Selling on Clients

"Do the four steps always lead to a sale?" the trainer asks. "Of course not. Not everyone buys, but when your agents have completed their conversations, customers have less indecision and fewer objections. And they buy more often and with greater commitment." The trainer lets this sink in and then adds: "As

Frank noticed earlier, these four steps—and especially the first two, Problem and Cost—*qualify* the customer. If customers won't take these initial steps, it is highly unlikely they will buy. Your sales agents need to learn these steps, so they don't waste their time with non-buyers."

You're convinced about the process, but you have a question that's been building inside you for the past hour. "This is very sophisticated stuff," you say, "and I know it's exactly what we need. But how do we help our sales agents put this into practice?"

"Great question," the trainer responds. "You can make this simple for your sales teams to learn. Don't present the DQ Sales® graph. Instead, use a series of four boxes to lay out the sequence, and walk them through it, like this—" The trainer quickly draws the diagram on the flip chart and explains the sequence of Problem, Cost, Solution, and Value (see Figure 4.7). Everyone writes the four words in the boxes in their workbooks, just as their agents will during their training.

"We find that many salespeople do better when you keep things simple. Don't teach them a model. Teach them the steps to take and why each step is important. Get them *practicing* the steps. Later on, after they've had experience using the steps, you can teach them the theory behind it.

"What makes this easy to learn and to follow in the field is a sales aid that we call a Sight Seller." The trainer holds up an A4-size spiral-bound booklet. It's a centimeter thick and has your company's branding on the outside. You helped put this together, and it's exciting to see it introduced.

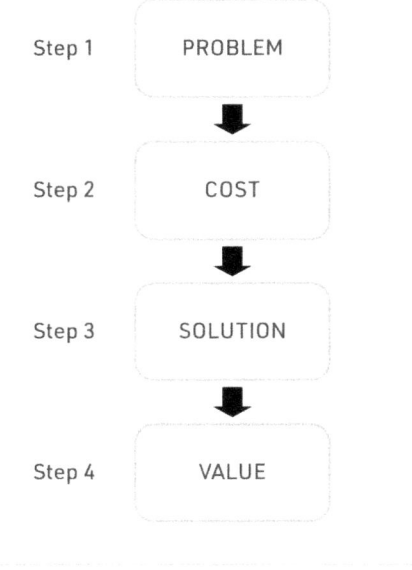

*Figure 4.7 The Four Stages of
the DQ Sales Conversation*

The trainer flips through it slowly as he talks. "These pages are full of pictures that sequentially illustrate the problems customers face, a way to calculate what those problems are costing them, how your product solves the problems, and a way to estimate the value your solution will bring." He hands out several copies of the Sight Seller, and your team breaks into small groups to look at it in more detail.

After a few minutes, the trainer continues. "You need to teach your sales agents how to use the Sight Seller just as I'm going to teach *you* now. I need a volunteer!" Several hands go up, and the trainer chooses Makena.

"I'll be the sales agent, and you be my prospect. I'll use the Sight Seller to guide our conversation, and you play along."

Makena smiles, enjoying the chance to be a customer. The trainer introduces himself as the agent and, starting with page one of the Sight Seller, walks her through the four-step conversation. She doesn't make it easy for him, but the trainer takes his time, refuses to do any "convincing," and guides her to make a decision that is just right for herself and her family.

After the demonstration, Frank exclaimed, "That was amazing! I was Makena's manager when she first joined the company. She was a great sales agent. She always talked with customers the way you just talked with her."

"Actually," Makena said with a grin, "I've had a hard time teaching my sales team to do what I naturally do well. This Sight Seller is going to do that. It's the framework we've been missing."

A switch flips in your brain, and you make a decision. This is the way you want your people to sell from now on. You don't know how you're going to do it, but you know you're going to make it happen. This could change *everything*.

> "I think our people could get up in the morning and do *this* for the rest of their lives. And be proud of it!"

And Gideon's final comment nails it for you. "I don't know about the rest of you, but I think our people could get up in the morning and do *this* for the rest of their lives. And be proud of it!"

PART THREE

TRANSFORMING THE PEOPLE WHO SELL

CHAPTER 5

ASLEEP AT THE WHEEL

Executive Summary

There's a fundamental, very human problem standing in the way of transforming the people who do your selling. It's the way the brain develops early in childhood. Around the age of five, our minds start to **automate** the way we think and act. **Living on autopilot** slowly replaces the ability to think outside the box, to notice when you're running in circles instead of moving forward and when you're operating on habit instead of real, free choice.

To turn off the autopilot takes both awareness and skill. And it's something that *everyone* can do, regardless of their cultural background or level of education.

We've been looking at the need to wake up and notice whatever selling behaviors you're caught in, the good habits as well as the bad ones. Now we turn to four **practices** that create the conditions in which you and your people can transform the way you sell—the way you think about it and the way you actually do it.

We've taught thousands of salespeople to raise their customer's DQ instead of pitching and persuading them. They prefer selling like this, *and* they are often surprised by how difficult it is to change their long-standing patterns of thought and action. This is *especially* true when it comes to sales and sales management.

When you accept that changing how your sales force thinks and acts is not a simple matter of learning a few techniques or simply working harder, you start thinking about what it will take to *transform* their approach to selling instead of just trying to improve it. And that realization raises a fundamental question: *why is it so difficult for people to change the way they think and act?*

We all had five uninterrupted years of *daily* transformation.

Transformative science points out that every one of us used to be *unconsciously masterful* at changing ourselves. We all had five uninterrupted years of *daily* transformation. If you want to watch this happening, spend time with a young child. Unless children are subjected to abusive conditions, their first five years are filled with one incredible change after another. They *naturally and easily* learn to move, to speak—several languages, if they're in the right environment—to sing, draw, dance, write, count, think for themselves, and boldly pursue what they want.

What changed between those early years and where we are now? What happened that made us so subject to habit and resistant to change? How did we willingly walk into prison, thinking it looked like home?

THE AUTOPILOT PARADOX

Modern neuroscience describes the development of what philosophers and theologians have long called the *human condition*. Around the age of five, our brains develop a self-reflective ability that literally starts *making up our minds* for us. It draws conclusions about everything that happens, tells us how to respond, and predicts what will happen if we don't follow its directions.[vi] If this is the first time you've heard about this mental development, it may seem too fantastic to be true. But spend some time listening to your own thinking, and you'll discover just how accurate it is.

All of us who have had small children can remember moments when, seemingly overnight, they became convinced that they could no longer do something that, up to that moment, they'd been doing naturally and with great enjoyment. "I can't draw," "I can't play piano," or "I'm no good at math" are the things parents start hearing from their six and seven-year-olds. Where did those conclusions come from? From the same place your salespeople are listening to when they say, "Closing is hard for me," or "I always get nervous when customers object."

Research estimates your brain produces 2,000–3,000 thoughts per hour, each requiring 1/25 of a second to influence your thinking and your behavior.[vii] This barrage of unnoticed input has been building ever since you were about five years old. By the time you were twenty, it had formed your personality and locked you into patterns of thought and action that *felt natural,* like you'd *always* been that way.

This conditioning process—which automates your behavior—actually has a positive purpose, which is probably why the brain evolved in this way. As fast as your mind works, it is still way too slow to respond to situations that call for an instant reaction—like a bus bearing down on you. There's a neurological circuit that bypasses this self-reflective part of your brain and goes straight to a motor center that causes you to jump to safety.

Even in nonthreatening situations, the operating circuitry of your brain—think RAM storage on a computer—just isn't big enough to consider consciously everything you do each day. For example, do you remember how challenging it was to learn to use your first smartphone? Instead of just having buttons numbered zero to nine and two more for Talk and End, you suddenly had to navigate an entirely new world of apps, icons, badges, digital communication, and a host of other options. Remember how complex that was? Now, you handle calling, texting, email, social media, gaming, and exploring the internet without even thinking about how to do it. It's become *automatic*, like so many of our daily activities.

Autopilot is very effective for certain everyday tasks, but it's extremely unhelpful when it comes to sales and sales management.

There is an upside to *living on autopilot*. It's a necessity for getting through the day. If you had to *think* about everything you did—walking, talking, opening doors—you'd get very little done. The brain, however, doesn't content itself with automating everyday tasks. It's an automating machine, and it tries to automate *everything*—including, for example, the way you think, feel, and react to customers and colleagues who look a certain way or say certain things. Autopilot is very effective for certain everyday tasks, but it's extremely unhelpful when it comes to sales and sales management.

Take a close look at your own sales teams. How many of these well-intentioned people react to surprises and challenges the same way they've always reacted? You can probably *predict* how each person is going to react when you increase their targets.

How much of your management time is devoted to trying to change the *circumstances* your team is dealing with because you can't figure out how to help them change their *reaction* to these circumstances? When salespeople and sales managers live on autopilot, they grow accustomed to—they feel comfortable with, they settle for—behaviors that actually *limit* their professional performance and reduce their personal fulfillment.

Fortunately, once you know what you're looking for, autopilot is easy to spot. Look for evidence of Einstein's definition of insanity, and you'll find lots of people who are "doing the same thing over and over again, expecting a different result."

Keep a sharp eye out for what's called polarity behavior: This is when salespeople or sales managers shift from one ineffective behavior to its opposite. They stick with something until it's overwhelmingly obvious it isn't working, they have a strong emotional reaction to failing, and then they do something quite different. When that doesn't work, they flip back to what they did before.

Here are two real-life examples.

A SALESPERSON ON AUTOPILOT

Agreeable

"Sophea," Kimsan called, as he burst through the front door of their small, well-kept home. "I got the job! Now I'm going to make some real money!" He had just completed his final interview with FireFriend, a clean cookstove company doing business in Cambodia. Recalling the hours his mother spent cooking family meals over an open fire, ruining her eyes and lungs, he added, "And I'm going to be doing something I really believe in."

"Well," she said, "that sounds wonderful."

"It certainly is," he said. And then he delivered the bad news: "I don't really like straight commission, and I'll have to work Saturdays every week—"

"Saturdays?" Sophea broke in. "But that's our time with the children—and no salary to count on?"

"I know," he replied. "But they said that everybody in sales works on that basis, so I figured I'd better just go along with it." He patted her on both shoulders. "It'll work out. You'll see."

The next day, Kimsan reported for work and was given a whirlwind training that focused on the technical features of the cookstove, using the company app to register buyers, as well as a few selling tips. That afternoon, he joined his new sales team in the field.

"Welcome," said Piseth, his manager. "Let's hit the road and make some sales!" Piseth spent the afternoon showing him the ropes, going door-to-door in the rural areas around Battambang. They made three sales. The next day, they worked together again, and they made four more sales. Piseth then announced that Kimsan's training was complete, and he was on his own.

When Piseth pocketed the commissions instead of splitting them with Kimsan, as he should have, Kimsan stayed quiet, not wanting to rock the boat. "I'll just make it up over the next couple of days," he told Sophea that evening. Sophea stayed quiet. She didn't want to rock the boat either.

Kimsan spent the next two weeks working from early morning until it was dark. He quickly mastered the FireFriend presentation, and he gave it to the many housewives and elders who were home during the day. Nearly always, their response was enthusiastic: "This is so easy to light, and there's no smoke— I love it!" But then would come the objections: "I don't have the money...can you come back?" or "I need to ask my husband first."

Kimsan kept smiling and making appointments to return, mentally calculating the commission he would make when they all said, "Yes." Very occasionally, some of them bought, but usually, the same housewife or elder would meet him at the door, make another excuse and ask him to return again. Sooner or later, they would just say, "No."

Feeling Frustrated and Conned

"I just keep hearing the same thing over and over," he said to Piseth when his manager pulled him aside to talk about his lack of sales. "People say they want it, but then they don't buy." He shook his head and let out a deep sigh. "I just don't understand. This is so frustrating! Why do they do that? It's like they're just trying to get rid of me, wear me down, but they just won't say so. I hate it when people do that."

"Well," Piseth said, "you're not making any money. You've got to do something different."

"I know that," Kimsan said, irritation creeping into his voice. "But what do you do when they just keep giving you one excuse after another?"

"I thought you wanted to be a salesperson," Piseth responded. "That means you've got to *sell*, not just roll over for them. If you don't think you can manage that, you probably need to find another line of work."

That did it. Something snapped inside. Enough was enough. No more Mr. Nice Guy. It was time to do what had to be done.

Aggressive

"I know what I'm going to do. I'm going to stop this nonsense and get people to tell me the truth," he said, muttering to himself. "The next time someone asks me to come back, I'm not going to take it. I know that some of the women have enough money to buy, and most of them can make their own decisions. They actually do that even when the husband is standing there with them!"

Armed with bravado, Kimsan set out to make some sales.

The next day, armed with bravado, Kimsan set out to make some sales. No longer would he take "I need to think about it" as an answer. It was clear that his product was really good, and it was unique. People would know if they wanted it or not. He just had to get them to say so.

He sped through his first demonstration. When a "come back later" objection arose, he was ready: "Don't you think the FireFriend is fabulous? Can't you see that it's worth the money because it will make you healthier?" he said. He could hear his voice getting louder. His customer stepped back a half-step and stammered, "Oh, yes, I do see that, really. But—" Here it comes, Kimsan thought, and he steeled himself. "Can't you just come back tomorrow when I have more time?" she asked.

Kimsan's words poured out before he could think about them. "No, I can't come back tomorrow." He was on a roll, and he kept going. "I'm too busy to come back because there are a lot of your neighbors who are ready to make a decision, and if you're not ready, there's nothing I can do about that." He felt bad for a moment and then added: "But here's my number if you decide you want it."

As he left, he mumbled to himself, "She'll never call." But as he walked out the door and up the street, he did feel more in control, more energetic. He thought to himself, "I'm a cobra, not a chicken."

Over the next several weeks, he pumped himself up before every presentation, and he kept being aggressive. It felt good, strong. Instead of being understanding, he attacked every objection; and he let customers see his dismay at their indecisiveness. He met each of their "excuses" with a clever reason to buy now. He even started shaming people for ignoring the health of their children and wasting their time and money on methods of cooking that he called "inferior" and "backward." He even goaded his customers into borrowing money from family and neighbors to pay the deposit that was required.

He was making more sales, but it was taking a toll on his peace of mind. "I'm being such a jerk," he said to his manager. Piseth replied, "Hey, that's the job," and, at the next sales meeting, he gave Kimsan a special award for "doing what it takes to win."

Another week passed. Kimsan noticed that he was running into more and more agitated conversations with his customers. He sensed that rumors about him were spreading throughout the commune. "When I introduce myself, some people are refusing to hear my presentation," he said to Piseth. "Don't worry about it," his manager replied. "You're my star. Just keep going."

That evening, when he arrived home—an hour after the children had gone to bed—Kimsan grabbed a beer and relaxed in the hammock. "You're not saying much," said Sophea. "Is everything okay?"

"This job is taking a lot out of me," was all he could offer. He didn't tell her about the angry husband who had hunted him down in the village, demanding a refund of the money his wife had given him earlier in the day. "She was in tears," he screamed at Kimsan. "She didn't want the stove. You pushed her into buying it. Shame on you!"

Two days later, Piseth pulled him aside. "That husband called me," he said. "And not just him. Several other customers as well. You're being too rough on everyone. You're getting them to buy, but many of them are canceling and demanding refunds. I have to claw back your commissions. And the big boss says he's beginning to worry that you're hurting our reputation."

Feeling Exhausted and Embarrassed

That night, Kimsan couldn't sleep. He couldn't let go of what Piseth had said. "I can't win," he thought. "I'm just trying to earn a living and get these people to do what's good for them and their families."

He lay in bed for another hour, fuming over the injustice of it all. Then, as he calmed down, he felt something different. It was an embarrassment. He remembered that husband screaming at him, and something inside woke up.

"He's right," he admitted to himself. "His wife really didn't want to buy. She was worried about the money involved and didn't look like she had it to spend." He took another deep breath and said to himself, "I did talk her into it…pushed her into it, actually." His face felt hot. He looked back over his demanding and aggressive conversations during the past month, and his mother's face appeared. He felt the guilt wash over him. There is no way that he would permit a salesperson to treat his mother the way he was treating many homemakers.

"I don't like what I'm doing," he said quietly. "No," he corrected himself, "I don't like *how* I'm doing it."

"I don't like it either," Sophea said. He didn't know she was awake. She didn't turn to face him, but she added, "You're not yourself, and it hurts me to see it."

Those words stung. And Kimsan decided that he had to change. No more pushing people around. "I don't have to do this to sell," he thought. "Why did I ever think that I had to behave like that? People buy from people they like, and I've always been someone others feel comfortable with."

He decided that starting tomorrow, he was going to put his best foot forward by being polite instead of disagreeable and returning as often as needed to get a sale. "If I'm patient enough," he thought, "they'll know I'm on their side, and they will buy." His decision made, he closed his eyes and went to sleep, knowing that tomorrow he would do things differently.

He didn't even realize he was back where he started (see Figure 5.1).

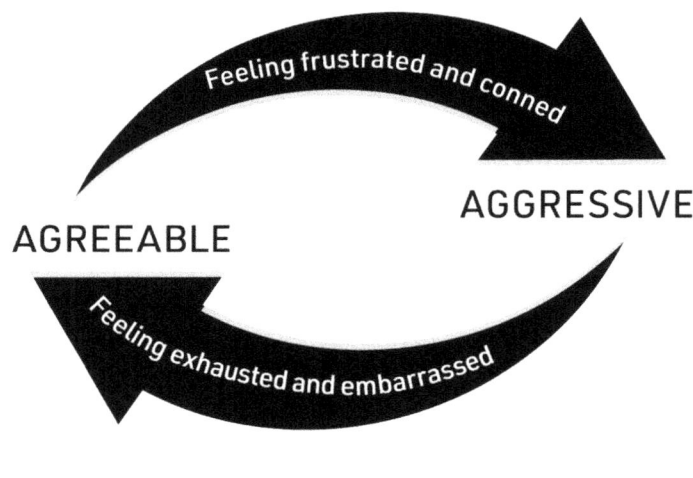

Figure 5.1 Salesperson on Autopilot

A SALES MANAGER ON AUTOPILOT

Directing

"Come into my office, Prakash; close the door behind you." Amit was Head of Sales for SecureHealth, an Indian company that provided low-cost health insurance for the rural poor. Manoj, Prakash's sales manager, reported directly to Amit, so this was an unusual situation.

"For the past six months," Amit began, "you've consistently been our top agent. I think it's time for you to help the rest of the team do what you do so well. Congratulations—you're our newest sales manager." Prakash wasn't completely surprised, but he thought this promotion would come later rather than sooner. Still, it was good to have his hard work rewarded.

"You'll take over for Manoj to see if you can do something with your old teammates. Frankly, they all need to learn how to work like you: disciplined, focused, and committed. Have a good weekend. You've got a big week coming up." Amit enthusiastically shook hands with Prakash, patted him on the shoulder, and started to usher him out of the office.

"Um, if I may, sir," Prakash started.

"Yes?"

"What's happening to Manoj?" Prakash asked.

"I'm letting him go," said Amit. "Always tough to do, but he just wasn't making things happen. It's up to you now. I'm counting on you to get your team into shape."

On the way home, Prakash was excited but also a little nervous. Becoming a manager was everything he had wanted, but he wondered how his former teammates would react to having him as their boss. Yes, Manoj wasn't very effective. He didn't really hold people's feet to the fire. But he was well-liked. Prakash knew he had to be tougher on everyone than Manoj had ever been. How would they take it?

The more he thought about it, the less he cared about their reaction. Most of them were masterful at cooking up excuses for why they didn't hit their targets. And it was his own sales figures that had been propping up the team's performance. Well, they were just going to have to step up and carry their weight.

At eight o'clock the next morning, Amit surprised the team by walking into the room. Three of the eight team members hadn't shown up yet, but that didn't slow Amit down.

"You've noticed, I'm sure, that Manoj isn't here this morning," he said in a voice ringing with strength. "He has left the company. That's all we're going to say about it, and I'm sure we all wish him well. Prakash here is your new manager. I'm sure that sales will pick up." Amit turned and walked out of the room, leaving a stunned silence in his wake.

Prakash cleared his throat and said, "Well, this is a shock for all of us, including me." No one laughed as he'd hoped they would. He sat up straighter and decided to go for it. "We're going to do things differently from now on, like starting on time." You could have heard a pin drop. The other three agents, who were just now wandering in, looked shell-shocked as Prakash gave each of them an icy stare.

"From now on," Prakash said, feigning a confidence he didn't feel, "we're not just going to meet our targets, we're going to smash them." Some agents looked away; others stared at him wide-eyed. He tried to present a compelling picture of the future. "You're all going to be top salespeople, I'm going to be a top manager, and we're all going to make a lot of money."

That brought a smile from a few of them. "But you're all going to work a *lot* harder." So much for the smiles.

He let that sink in. No one said a word. He decided to lay down the law about work habits: "There will be no more excuses. Be at work on time, every day. Work ten solid hours and deliver 20 presentations. That's what I've done for two years, and that's why I'm sitting in this chair. If I can do it, you can too, and I expect nothing less."

More silence. Prakash continued. "We're going to meet every morning, and I'll talk to each of you several times a day until you start hitting your targets," Prakash asserted. "In three months, we are going to be the top sales team in the company." Prakash looked at his former teammates and asked, "Are there any questions?"

Neeraj tried to lighten the mood: "I guess we're all going to be busier from now on." No one laughed. Prakash replied, "Indeed, you are. Let's get going." The team left for the field with more urgency than ever before.

Two hours later, Neeraj was in the middle of a presentation when his phone rang. "Excuse me," he said to the couple with whom he'd been speaking. "This is my new boss. I have to take it."

"How many presentations so far today?" Prakash blurted out. When Neeraj responded with a low number, trying to work in the fact that, at the moment, he was actually in the middle of one, Prakash launched into a lecture on how to get his number up: make his demos shorter, move faster between houses, and be more committed to the presentation target. When Neeraj returned to his customer, he couldn't remember where he'd left off.

Neeraj sheepishly reported that he'd missed his targets, and Prakash delivered a 20-minute lecture on work habits.

As the day progressed, Prakash called him twice more and texted him four times. At the end of the day, Neeraj sheepishly reported that he'd missed his targets, and Prakash delivered a 20-minute lecture on work habits.

After the first week, the sales team was talking a lot among themselves. "Man, things are really different around here, and I'm not liking it," Naveen whispered into Anup's ear before the start of the morning meeting, which by now was being regarded by everyone as "more of the same." "Prakash is hounding everyone," Anup responded. "I heard he was actually in the field yesterday, selling with Ishaan, and he kept taking over the demo. Ishaan's really upset about it."

When Prakash entered the room, he noticed that *everyone* stopped talking. They were all there, on time, but it wasn't a fun place to be. The team was making more sales, but no one seemed particularly happy about it. The enjoyment had disappeared, just like Manoj.

Prakash was beginning to wonder if he was pushing his troops too hard. Sales figures had risen during the first couple of months, and he was getting praise from on high, but he could tell that things were slowing down. Complaints were increasing, and, Prakash had to admit to himself, he'd be complaining too if he were the complaining type. Some handwriting was appearing on the wall.

Feeling Exhausted and Trapped

Over the weekend, he heard from his wife. "You've got to stop working like this, Prakash," Priya said, "or you're going to burn out. I can't think of the last time you took a day off." He knew she was right, but he didn't see any options. His team was growing more and more resistant to his input. As a result, he was spending even more time delivering his messages about right effort, good habits, and full responsibility.

"It will get better," he said, not actually believing his own words. Priya took a deep breath, and he knew something big was coming. "Quit kidding yourself, Prakash. You're married to your job more than you are to me." That hurt. And he was still feeling the ache when he returned to work Monday morning.

"Where's Vinay?" said Ishaan the next morning. Their top producer was missing. Prakash felt hollow inside; he had worked harder with Vinay than anyone else, and he had turned Vinay into a top seller. He looked at Deepa, a long-time friend of Vinay's, and he noticed that Deepa wouldn't look at him.

"Deepa?" Prakash asked.

"He quit," Deepa said. "He texted me fifteen minutes ago. I thought you knew."

Neeraj added, "I was afraid of this. Two days ago, he was blowing off steam. He ranted about how he was a grown-up and didn't need a parent watching his every move and trying to run his life. He said he might just look for another job, but

I didn't take him seriously. I mean, he was doing so well here." Prakash looked at his phone. There it was: the text message from Vinay. Short and not so sweet. He was gone.

Prakash struggled through the rest of the meeting. Everyone was deflated. He cut the meeting short and went to Amit's office to break the news about his best salesperson leaving.

"I worked so hard to help him be number one," Prakash said to Amit, "and this is the thanks I get." He was hoping for sympathy, but Amit wasn't the type. "Prakash," he said. "Let's face it. You've been riding them way too hard. I haven't said anything because I wanted to give you room to play out what you thought you had to do. But I've been hearing complaints around the office."

Prakash was furious. Amit had been the one telling him to "shape up" the team. Before he could say anything, Amit continued. "Listen, you've got to watch very carefully what you do now. This sort of defection can destroy a sales team. You've just gutted their ability to hit their team target for the quarter. Who might be the next to leave? What are you going to do to get people back on your side?"

After a few more cliches, including the one about catching more flies with honey than vinegar, Amit sent Prakash home for the rest of the day to "think long and hard about how you're going to repair the damage."

"Maybe I've made a big mistake," he said to Priya that afternoon. "And you're right, I've been driving myself—and my team—way too hard." Priya wrapped her arms around him and, to her credit, didn't offer platitudes or advice. Instead, she said, "Looks like you've got to do some things differently. Let's talk about what they might be."

Priya had worked in HR for several years. She knew how to help people think deeply about what they were doing. Over the next few hours, she sat with Prakash as he developed a new approach to managing his people.

"I was great at selling," he told her. "I was disciplined, smart, and kept learning as I worked. And I didn't do all that because someone pushed me; I did it because I *wanted* to. And the one thing that Manoj did right as a manager was *trust* me to get on with it. *That's* what I've not been doing right. No wonder Vinay quit. No wonder others are complaining. That's going to change, right now."

That evening, he sat down to dinner with his family for the first time in weeks. After putting the children to bed, Prakash called on Priya's expertise to plan a different approach to sales management. From now on, he was getting off everyone's back—including his own.

Trusting

The next morning, the team was surprised when Prakash opened the sales meeting with an apology. He took responsibility for the part he had played in Vinay's decision to quit; he acknowledged that, without Vinay's sales, hitting the team target for the quarter would be hard. "But I don't want you to worry about that," he said. "I want you to give it your best shot, and we'll live with the results." A couple of his agents look relieved; the rest seemed wary.

"I trust you," said Prakash. "You've all worked hard—yes, I pushed you to work hard, *too* hard at times. But the good news is that you're ready to go to the next level." Prakash paused for a moment. The group looked cautious but curious. His strategy was working.

"You know what to do, and I trust you to do it."

"This is our last daily sales meeting. You don't need to meet five times a week anymore. You know what to do, and I'm going to trust you to do it. We'll meet once a week, on Mondays. We'll set our targets for all six days, and you'll set your own schedule for the week. No more daily reporting of your activity. You're all adults. You can track your own numbers and give them to me at the end of the week. You need to do what you *want* to do instead of what I tell you to do.

"Now," he said, "I'm going to step out of the room. Talk together as a team, and decide if you're willing to step up to this way of operating. I'll be back in ten minutes." As the door closed behind him, he heard conversation starting. A good sign.

When he returned, the group was quiet as he took his seat. Prakash smiled and said, "I'm assuming that, since you're all here, you've decided to go for it. Wonderful. Let's take the next step. A mature sales team doesn't need to be told what to do. I'm convinced that, when each of you is free to do your best, we will sell far more than the company is asking for. So, from now on, you're going to set your own targets, based on what you really *want* to do. Write down your sales goals for the next month and give them to me as you leave the meeting."

It didn't take people long to set sales goals for themselves. As they left the meeting, Prakash, noticed that they not only seemed relieved, they actually looked excited. He overheard Deepa say to Neeraj, "I don't know what he's been smoking, but he's seen the light!"

Sales that week were the best since Prakash had taken over as manager. On Friday evening, he said to Priya, "I can't believe it…it's actually working! They're really going for it, on their own. I didn't spend one minute in the field this week. What a relief!" Free from requirements to meet, report, and discuss how things were going, Prakash *and* his team were happier and more productive.

"I don't know why I ever thought I had to push them so hard," Prakash said. "This is *so* much easier. And some of the team are voluntarily sending me their numbers at the end of the day. I don't even have to speak with them. I was worried when the targets they chose were short of what I've got to produce, but, at this rate, we'll do great!"

At Monday's sales meeting, spirits were high. Prakash followed his new plan to avoid putting people on the spot and challenging their thinking as he'd done in the past. Instead, he asked the group to talk together about how they were selling: how they decided which doors to knock on, what they actually said during their demos, how they tracked their activity and measured their progress.

He noticed that most of the team weren't thinking very deeply about what they were doing. They certainly didn't seem to remember everything he'd taught them. And they were starting to say and do things in the field that Prakash didn't actually think would work. But he kept quiet, confident that they would learn on their own. After all, that was the point.

That week, sales leveled off. And over the next several weeks, sales continued to decline. A serious revenue gap was emerging, but he worked hard to stay positive and supportive. When some of the team did ask for help, he spent these one-to-one meetings patiently listening to their struggles and trying to "coach" them into figuring out what to do instead of just telling them. *That* was hard work. And it was a bit depressing to notice afterward that, when it came to sales results, nothing much changed.

What *did* change, however, gave him concern. Discipline was slipping, complaints and excuses were rising, and there were numerous signs that his team just wasn't fully committed to what they were doing. Agents were leaving the office later in the morning and returning earlier from the field. They were spending more time phoning and texting and less time knocking on doors.

One day, he discovered three team members hanging around the office in the middle of the day, drinking tea. "The weather was terrible, people didn't want to talk to us—we were just wasting our time out there," one of them said. Another added, "We knew you'd understand." That got his attention.

Half an hour later, he learned that this behavior had gotten Amit's attention as well. "I don't know what you're doing, Prakash," he said, as he closed the door, sealing them once again inside his office, "but sales aren't improving—in fact, they're getting worse in a hurry. You're headed for trouble."

Prakash started to explain, but Amit wasn't interested. "The word around the office is that you've gone soft," he said. "Your team is setting their own targets? Are you crazy? What about *our* targets? What are you going to do about your team's sales? There's no way you'll close the gap this quarter. What are your guys actually *doing* out there?" Prakash's stomach sank. He couldn't honestly answer the question. He felt cold inside.

Feeling Frustrated and Out of Control

That night he confided in Priya. "I'm going crazy. This isn't working. I knew better than to try this. I don't know if they're stupid or just lazy, but I *do* know they're taking advantage of me. *That* has got to stop." He felt his heart racing and his face heating up.

"At least, when I was running things my way, I knew what they were doing and what had to be fixed. Now, I know nothing. I don't have hard data anymore. You can't fix what you can't see. And you can't treat people as responsible adults if they're not actually responsible adults! I gave all of them the room they needed to do things their own way, and not only did they let me down, they let themselves down."

He took a big breath, and he heard the sadness in his own voice. "It was a mistake to manage them the way I like to be managed. If I had a team of people like me, then it would work. But the truth is, they're not like me. They're not disciplined, and they're not self-motivated. I've been a fool to treat them as if they were."

> "It was a mistake to manage them as I like to be managed."

Priya said, "So, what are you going to do?"

"It's time to quit pretending they can do what they want and hit their sales targets," he said. "I've got to take control of the situation, starting tomorrow." Prakash paused a moment and realized that, for the first time in weeks, he felt completely at peace. Now he knew what to do. He opened his laptop and sent an email to his team, instructing everyone to be in the office the next morning at eight o'clock.

Daily sales meetings were back (see Figure 5.2).

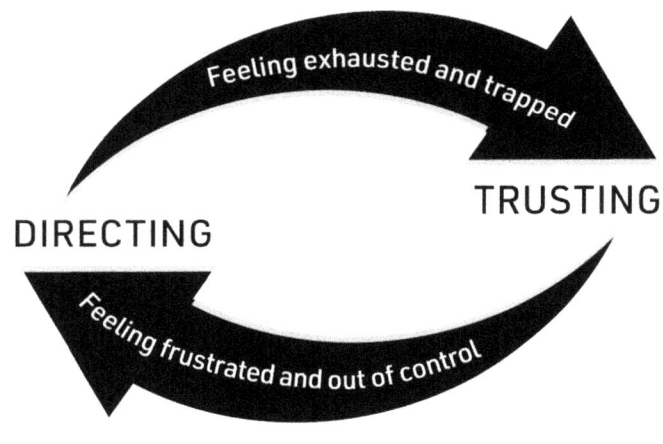

Figure 5.2 Sales Manager on Autopilot

We expect that, somewhere in these two stories, you can see yourself and your teams. Kimsan's cycle is an example of how sales agents often bounce back and forth from *being understanding and agreeable with their customers to being aggressive and putting on the pressure in order to get a sale.* Prakash's cycle similarly describes the two behaviors that sales managers often adopt: being *demanding and directive* or sitting back and trusting that things will go well.

The point here is that *all* of these behaviors—and flipping back and forth between them—are examples of *automaticity*. When one strategy backfires, people on autopilot don't have the breathing room to stop, learn, and try something *really* new. Instead, they revert to what they know. They default to habit, even when *that* automatic behavior didn't work before. Talk about insanity.

And that takes us to an insight from transformational science that our clients have found extremely helpful as they lead the change process in their companies.

NEVER TRUST A HABIT

We've spent this chapter looking at the very human problem of falling into unconscious, automatic behavior. As one of our early transformational trainers said to us, "It's not your fault that you 'go automatic,' but it is your responsibility to do something about it."

With that in mind, consider this definition of a habit:

A settled disposition or tendency to act in a certain way, especially one acquired by frequent repetition of the same act until it becomes almost or quite involuntary.[viii]

And here is a neuroscientist commenting on how the brain works:

Brains are in the business of gathering information and steering behavior appropriately. It doesn't matter whether consciousness is involved in the decision-making. And most of the time, it's not.[ix]

And some traditional wisdom that puts it metaphorically and bluntly:

Man is asleep. Must he die before he wakes?[x]

When it comes to selling, it's obvious that effective habits are better than ineffective ones. There are truckloads of books on personal and professional development aimed at helping people establish healthy, productive behaviors. But transformational science raises a caution flag about seeking to develop *habits*.

The fundamental problem with habitual behavior is that it's *unconscious, not chosen.* Once you stop choosing what you do, you lose the ability to choose something *different.* You lose what you were born with—the ability to change when you want to. Regaining that *natural ability* to transform yourself is the key to high performance—not just in sales, but in any pursuit.

And the first step in regaining that ability is to *notice* when you've fallen into autopilot, *refuse* to revert to previous habits, and *choose* your next step based on what really matters to you.

> Once you stop choosing what you do, you lose the ability to choose something *different*.

That's why our clients focus on developing the right *practices* instead of better habits. You *choose* practices; they don't become automatic. And if you find yourself doing a helpful practice out of habit, it's a good idea to stop, take a breath, locate your purpose for what you're about to do, and *choose* the practice or *choose* to do something else.

This focus on *making purposeful choices,* moment-by-moment, is what wakes us up from living on autopilot. It brings clearer thinking, confident decisions, and wiser actions. You access what you lost early in life: freedom, flexibility, and boldness.

Gaining this access is actually a very simple process. It involves learning how to bring what's called "present-moment awareness" to whatever you're doing. This is a skill that can be learned, and when you practice it, a natural, inherent *brilliance* emerges. It sounds a bit magical—and it actually *feels* a bit magical when it happens—but in fact, it's a natural process that neuroscience refers to as "*developing new neural pathways.*" *It's what happens when* you rise to the challenge of transforming yourself and the way you sell.

That's what this part of the book is all about: how to put transformational science to work for you and your sales force. You don't have to be concerned about the number of ineffective habits your people already have or how long they've had them. And it's not a matter of hiring more educated or sophisticated people. The practices are simple to do and call on the common sense and shared humanity that people around the world possess.

Get the right behavior in place—the simple, clear practices that *require* people to become *awake and aware,* to turn off their autopilot and make a free choice—and the *activity of selling becomes a transformational force* within your entire company.

Structure your sales process around this possibility, and some very interesting things start happening.

We want to stress that these practices are neither exotic nor difficult. And when your sales managers start living them and require your salespeople to follow their lead, they create the conditions in which transformation not only happens sporadically but continues to happen week after week. Six months into her sales transformation program, Esther Altorfer said, "I was surprised by how much the material actually centered on the *personal* development of us as human beings. It has changed our previous approach to selling, and it's changed the way our senior team makes decisions about where we're taking the company."

Let's use the transformational formula—R=A+C+E™—to look at four fundamental practices that can transform your team's performance:

- **Aiming your brain** at the inputs that generate the sales *results* you seek

- **Mastering your *attitude*** to create consistent, proactive performance

- **Generating compelling conversations** by developing the *competence* to lead people to informed, committed action

- **Developing your people** through a consistent system of sales *execution* that creates ongoing learning

CHAPTER 6

AIM YOUR BRAIN

Executive Summary

To utilize the transformational formula—R=A+C+E—you need to discover the results you **really** want to create. Start with your professional objectives, especially your sales targets. But don't stop there. Dig deeper for the *wants-under-the-wants*—what **really** matters to you.

This is how you take charge of **aiming your brain**. Either you control this process, or it will control you (and you know where that leads). Master the practice of aiming, and you'll be amazed by how your brain starts working for you instead of against you.

When you direct your aim at developing the DQ of your customers, you'll figure out how to develop a Sight Seller (see chapter 4) that your sales agents can use to keep the selling conversation on track. And you'll identify the practices your sales managers must undertake to keep developing the ability of their teams (see chapter 9).

When you have done this, you will have a process that your sales force can follow, step-by-step, customer-by-customer, to meet and then exceed their sales targets in a genuinely sustainable way.

"Would you tell me, please, which way I ought to go from here?" "That depends a good deal on where you want to get to," said the Cat. "I don't much care where—" said Alice. "Then it doesn't matter which way you go," said the Cat.[xi]

Kevin Starr said it clearly when he described his foundation's purpose: "We're about scaling impact, not organizations." Impact is the point, behavior change is often the measurement, and selling well makes it happen. You've got to sell well in order to do good.

You've got to sell well in order to do good.

The "R" in the transformational formula represents results (see Figure 2.1). At the end of each month, quarter, and year, you'll either have the sales *results* that bring the impact you wanted, or you'll have all the *reasons* you couldn't get them. Results or reasons: you can't have both.

Sometimes it's hard for social entrepreneurs to embrace the need to sell. "I understand their difficulty," said Lisa Mikkelsen. "I always said that I was a *people* person, not a *sales*person." Erica Mackey and Beth Szymanski reported that, for most of the daycare providers they are training to run successful businesses, "the concept of selling is intimidating." When Karen Genzink was in the field as a WRP consultant, she observed that "social entrepreneurs are usually highly educated in everything *except* selling. Often, they don't really understand how to do it, and they count on someone else to make it happen."

We're suggesting that not only can social entrepreneurs understand selling, they *must* do so if they are to develop an effective selling system that aligns with their principles and values. The standard for selling is actually *higher* in social enterprises than it is for commercial ventures. Selling practices and mission must *both* be considered, respected, and fully integrated. Otherwise, your brand is going to suffer.

The way your company sells will determine the way you are perceived by the market in which you're operating: a market defined by the customers you serve and the communities in which these customers live. With apologies to the King James Bible, you might say, "As you sell, so shall you reap."

When you understand that the fulfillment of your mission depends not only on how *much* you sell but also on the *way* you sell, then you start bringing your best creative thinking to the task of designing a selling system that is uniquely suited to your goods and services. To do this, it helps to begin with what we've learned from transformational science about you and your brain.

AIMING YOUR BRAIN

The Cheshire Cat was right. If you don't know your destination, it doesn't much matter which way you go. The situation is slightly more complicated for your sales force. The destination is probably well-identified; they have sales targets, right? What's probably not so clear is the path to hit those targets—how to avoid wasting your time and squandering your resources.

Before we talk about that path—the specific activities your sales force needs to do in order to sell well and stay on mission—it will help to look at what we as human beings are up against when we attempt to figure out what to do and when to do it.

Let's start with you and the members of your leadership team. Undoubtedly, all of you have explored self-management skills: how to manage information flow, develop priorities, handle to-do lists, email, and the like. A lot of this work is good, even brilliant.[xii] A transformational perspective, however, focuses on a more fundamental challenge that must be dealt with *first* if self-management skills are to be used effectively.

This deeper challenge concerns a critical neurological fact that you may not be fully aware of: your brain drives you in many different directions, and you don't always know that it's doing it! As one of our early mentors once asked, "Who's aiming your brain, and what are you going to do about it?"

The first book we read about this was published in 1960.[xiii] It asserted that the human brain, weighing about three pounds and containing billions of neurons and trillions of synapses, is built to *fulfill commands*, to be *aimed* at some goal or objective.

This is easy to demonstrate. Take a moment and imagine a purple elephant with pink polka dots. Did you notice that you could *see* this elephant in your imagination? Your brain created that mental image in response to the instruction.

This process happens automatically. And, as we've already mentioned, it's how our minds mislead us, starting around the age of five: interpreting what happens, telling us what to do, and generating anxiety and fear about the future. You can watch this happen in real time. Set a timer for five minutes. Close your eyes and pay attention to your own thoughts as they fire off, wander around, and pull you this way and that.

Competing for Your Attention

An esoteric teacher was talking to a friend who was arguing that human beings had free will.[xiv] "Ah," said the teacher. "I'll show you free will." He drew a circle with many squares inside it, each of which contained a capital I.

"A person wakes up in the morning, and one of his I's says, 'I want to go to work.' Immediately, another I speaks up, and says, 'I want to stay in bed.' Two minutes later, another one pipes up, 'I'm hungry.' Another says, 'I'm too fat. I need to skip breakfast.' It goes on like that all day long. *That's* what people call free will."

This is the autopilot at work. And quietly, underneath your conscious awareness, *this* is what's aiming your brain! This is how we lose the power of choice and fall into autopilot without knowing it's happening.

This automatic aiming goes on morning, noon, and night for every human being, regardless of their education, culture, professional experience, or personal circumstances. *This* is what pulls your salespeople and sales managers off track by providing *other* targets for them to pursue—other things that, for the moment, seem important and valuable but which ultimately interfere with fulfilling their sales objectives.

You may have sales agents who believe they are committed to a particular sales target but whose neurological circuitry is actually *more* committed to earning money any way they can, getting promoted, or looking like they're busy when they're not—all of which pull their focus and energy away from what they need to do to actually sell well. You may have sales managers who believe they are committed to helping their teams get good at selling but whose unnoticed thinking is actually *more* committed to keeping family members on the payroll, protecting their status as "managers," and avoiding going out into the field.

You and they are very aware of the fact they are not keeping their commitments to your company, but what's harder to see is all of the *automatic aiming that draws* them away from their intended path, keeps them from thinking clearly, and tempts them into unnecessary and ineffective activity. Unless you address this very human tendency to slip into autopilot, the typical solutions of goalsetting, time management, and tracking systems will not create long-term behavior change in your sales force.

When it comes to increasing the effectiveness of your sales force, the science of transformative learning is extremely clear: if you want to make a substantive, permanent change in the way you think and act, you've got to *begin* by learning how to aim your brain instead of letting it aim itself.

Aim your brain instead of letting it aim itself.

You do this by discovering how to access what is traditionally called your Deep Desire. "This was one of the most surprising and helpful parts of the program," said Jim Taylor.[8] "The skill of staying in touch with your 'why'—knowing when you've got hold of it and when you don't. This is *essential* for salespeople and their managers."

UNLEASHING DEEP DESIRE

The word *unleashing* is dramatic. We chose it because discovering what you *really* want often brings an explosion of inventiveness, originality, and boldness. It *feels* dramatic.

We're thinking of Ade, a senior vice president who managed the national sales activity of her Nigerian company that sells water purifiers to the rural poor. She was in the second day of her live video training with her senior sales team. The group had explored the *many I's* that interfered with leading their sales teams—the mental *aims* that distracted them from what they needed to do. They were intrigued by the concept of Deep Desire as a way to increase their ability to focus and direct themselves. Ade wasn't shy about speaking up, and she volunteered to demonstrate the process.

She took a moment to quiet her thinking and place her full attention on her quarterly sales target. Then, she started to talk about why she *really* wanted to hit it.

"I want to be the leader of a team that doesn't just hit targets, but exceeds them," she said.

"And you want that," said the trainer, "because you want…what?"

---

8   Founder of Proximity Designs in Myanmar.

Ade paused a moment, then continued. "Because doing that would require me to *keep* developing my team, creating a real *learning organization* that is hungry to see just how successful they can become."

"And you want that because you want…?"

"I want a big bonus!" She was greeted with lots of laughter and some applause from the team.

The trainer followed her line of thinking. "And you want a big bonus because you want…?"

Ade paused even longer, seemingly surprised by the question. "Well," she started slowly, "I *do* want more money…" The trainer stayed silent; the pattern for Ade to follow was now obvious. "…and I want more money because I want the finest education possible for my children…to introduce them to the wider world and their part in making it better."

The group was still and silent, eyes looking directly at their screens, waiting for Ade to continue. This depth of conversation was unusual and strangely welcome.

"And you want that for your children because you want…"

"I joined this company seven years ago," Ade said. "I thought I'd only be here a year and then move on. But," she took a breath, "what we're doing here matters…a lot…to many people." Everyone waited for her to continue, sensing there was more to come.

"And I not only want my children to grow up in a better world, I want them to be proud of me and follow my example."

Ade then shifted to what she wanted professionally, about becoming even more of a leading figure in the company. "I want everyone who works with me to look back on the time we had together and know that I gave it my best."

At that point, she ran out of words. Her silence was eloquent. Everything felt *bigger*. Ade had accessed her Deep Desire. She knew it, the group knew it, and the brightness in her eyes confirmed it.

The trainer asked one last question. "Now, as you sit here, feeling what you're feeling, what is your very next step—the very next thing you're going to do to move toward those things you most deeply want?"

Ade thought a moment and said, "On Monday, following this training, I'm going to gather us all together and develop a concrete plan for implementing what we've learned. We will *not* lose 87% of what we're learning here. We're going to change things, permanently."

FOCUSING ON THE INPUTS

Discovering what you *really* want is the first step in *aiming*. Your Deep Desire not only fuels the journey toward your professional goals, but it also strengthens your ability to *turn off* your autopilot. You spend more time aiming your brain, and your brain spends less time aiming you.

Take a few minutes and try it right now. Pick a goal that matters to you. Find a place where you can be quiet and completely focused for a few minutes. Put pen to paper and start digging for why you *really* want to achieve that goal.

A simple statement starts the process: "I want…" Take that statement deeper by completing the sentence with, "And I want that because I want..." You can alter the words as you go: "I want that because my intention is to;" "my purpose is to;" "what I want to create is." Just keep digging, breathing, feeling—see where it takes you.

This is a simple but profound exercise.[xv] It puts you on the solid ground of what Jim Taylor referred to as the *why* behind your goal. Standing on this ground brings resolve, focus, and, strangely enough, *confidence*. Once your *why* is in place, you're ready for the next step: aiming at the right things, the *inputs* that deliver the *output.*

Aim at the right things: the *inputs* that deliver the *output*.

Why is this important? Because you really can't *make* the output happen! This is especially true in sales, where so many things—market conditions, economics, the circumstances driving customer decisions—are simply out of your control. What you *can* control is a rather narrow but remarkably powerful list of practices. They fall into the three categories you will remember from chapter 2:

- Attitude—staying Above-the-Line as you work (more about this below)

- Competence—mastering the skills you need to succeed

- Execution—doing the right things at the right time with the right people

Keep these categories in mind as you read the rest of the book. We'll share the key practices and activities that create the conditions for transforming the way you sell and the people who do it for you. That will help you figure out the specific inputs you want your sales force to learn, track, and eventually master.

Aiming at the right inputs generates a remarkable transition for everyone in the process. Sometimes, you notice the results right away. At other times, a few weeks may pass before you realize your anxiety has gone down, your confidence has risen, and your actions are decisive and effective. Knowing your *why* and focusing on the right *inputs* opens the door to peak performance.

When your sales managers get good at doing this with *everyone* in the sales force, and when they *keep* doing it through times of success and times of failure, you will see a remarkable change take place in everyone's ability to learn new behaviors. They'll do their jobs because they *want* to, not because they *have* to—and *that* is the source of initiative, boldness, and brilliance.

Are there any drawbacks to proceeding in a way that is so fundamentally transformational? Of course. It's not easy, it's not a quick fix, and some people will quit on you. We happen to think that's good news, by the way. It eliminates a lot of wear and tear on your HR department.

The one big drawback is that you and everyone else are going to speak your mind more often. You won't be quite as easy to work with as you were before. You'll push back more on people, policies, and procedures that block your movement forward. No matter what arises, you'll press to find a way to stay on course because now it matters. As you might guess, we don't actually regard this as a drawback—especially in a mission-driven organization. It's actually the only way great impact gets delivered.

Now, let's take a look at the key transformational practices in the areas of attitude, competence, and execution. We start with the most critical skill of the bunch: how your people can manage their attitude—their state of mind—moment-by-moment as they work. In Figure 2.1, this skill is represented by the fulcrum (the pivot point) in the leverage diagram because it is the quickest, surest, and most effective way for people to turn off their autopilot, engage their natural brilliance, and generate the results they're aiming at.

CHAPTER 7

MASTER YOUR ATTITUDE

Executive Summary

Attitude is central to success. You can learn to manage it moment-by-moment as you work. When you do, you access a profound and naturally high-performing capacity within yourself.

From ages zero to five, you lived in that state nearly full-time. Now, as an adult, you can use Split Attention to lift yourself out of autopilot into the present moment **as you work**. Combine it with discovering your Deep Desire, and you can spend a lot more of your professional hours Above-the-Line instead of Below-the-Line. The impact is immediate and compelling.

Split Attention is an inherent part of our transformational selling practices. In the next chapter, you will see how to use it while leading customers and colleagues in conversations that generate understanding, agreement, and committed action.

*The purpose...is to help you find what you think
you already have, namely free will, intelligence, and
self-consciousness. I expect you to find this idea preposterous.*[xvi]

Attitude is the "A" in the transformational formula, R=A+C+E™ (see Figure 2.1). Learning to manage it moment-by-moment is the fastest and surest way to raise the level of your salespeople's performance. For most sales leaders, however, that is easier said than done. As one of our commercial clients, a senior sales VP, said: "Attitude is everything. I know when it's right, but I don't know what to do when it's wrong."

This is where the insights and practices of transformative learning are invaluable. They demystify mindset—what causes it and what changes it. Master the ability to help people change their state of mind, and you become a leader who *builds* your people instead of organizing their activity and driving them to perform.

The first step in becoming such a leader is to face an unpleasant, even brutal truth—a truth that does indeed sound *preposterous*. Most people spend a *staggering* amount of time on autopilot. People who haven't discovered their own automaticity find this hard to believe. But anyone who's attempted to change the way they work, or the way their direct reports work, knows how difficult it is for people to *notice* their ineffective behavior, *admit* it's not working, and *change* what they do.

When people are stuck on autopilot, those are exactly the three things they can't do. Instead, they *explain* why their actions should have worked, *blame* someone or something else for why they didn't, and *repeat* the behavior, hoping this time they will succeed.

In fact, we are so used to working on autopilot that it often takes a shock to the system to get our attention. We *do* receive these shocks—the surprises, disappointments, and failures we didn't want or expect—we just don't know how to *use* them to wake up, turn off the autopilot, and choose to do something new. This ability to wake up is what we started losing around age five. Fortunately, we can find it again. And the desire to do so explains why a number of companies in the West are experimenting with mindfulness training.

It's taken nearly six decades for modern business leaders to "discover" the value of a quiet mind and a calm center. This is an invaluable asset when it comes to navigating the challenges and pressures of the business world, especially the world of sales.

But Eastern practices can be a difficult fit for the workplace. Mindfulness teaching usually follows its Buddhist origins, relying on one form or another of meditation: sitting quietly for a period of time and focusing your attention inward. This is a valuable practice, but it has significant limitations in the work environment. Often, the good feeling generated by thirty minutes of meditation fails to last through the first coffee break of the day. And when your attitude takes a dive in the middle of a conversation, you can't say, "Excuse me. I need to meditate for a while so that I can stand being in the same room with you!"

To successfully *integrate* mindful awareness into daily work, you need to develop two skills. First, you've got to *become aware* you're on autopilot;

> "Excuse me. I need to meditate for a while so that I can stand being in the same room with you!"

then, you have to *turn it off* without withdrawing from whatever you're doing or whomever you're with. Master these two skills, and your professional performance will increase exponentially. They truly are what has been called an "open secret," available to anyone who wants to discover it.[xvii]

Anushka Ratnayake, for example, tells her sales staff that they must learn how to increase self-awareness and self-management if they're going to overcome the obstacles they face. "It's how you get control over yourself, so you're not controlled by external events such as weather, resistant farmers, and other daily disappointments." Klann Mab, the national operations manager for iDE Cambodia's sanitation marketing program, said, "I was the first person in my company to learn this skill, and I teach it to *everybody*—including my own family." [xviii]

Paying attention to your attitude, and noticing when you've fallen into autopilot, isn't difficult. But you do have to know what to look for.

ABOVE-THE-LINE AND BELOW-THE-LINE

Grace, one of our trainers, was teaching attitude management to a cohort of social entrepreneurs and their front-line sales managers in the UK. This was the management training that usually takes place ahead of the training for sales agents. The group wanted to learn how to manage their own attitudes so they could lead-by-example during the subsequent training for their teams.

Grace opened the session with a question. "We've all had periods of time—an hour, a few hours, maybe even an entire day—in which our attitude, our state of mind, was really *up,*" she said. "When was the last time that happened for you? What was it like?"

The answers came quickly. She wrote them on the top half of the flip chart page: *productive, creative, strong, energetic, sharp, fun, relaxed, focused, intuitive.*

"And when those *up* times included challenges, difficulties, or issues to handle?"

The group offered more answers: "The problem didn't seem that big," "I could always figure out something to do."

Grace's next question evoked their emotions: "And how do you *feel* when you're up?" They described this state of mind at length, using words that included: *powerful, in control, centered, flexible, and confident.* A sense of awareness entered the room, and the trainer let the silence linger.

Then she asked, "Now, what's it like to work when you're feeling *down* instead of up?" A new set of words and phrases came forward, and the trainer wrote them on the lower half of the page: *struggling, confused, frustrated, angry, zero patience, I wasn't sure what to do, nothing seemed to work, I couldn't focus on the problem, I kept getting distracted, and I couldn't see any options.*

Grace kept collecting their descriptions of everyday experiences—feelings, thoughts, and behaviors—and writing them on the flip chart, either on the top half of the page or the bottom half. She allowed enough time for their awareness to grow, and then she picked up a thick, black marker and drew a horizontal line across the middle of the page, separating the two groups of words.

"Attitude really isn't more complicated than this," she said. "Every minute of every day, you're either *above* this line or *below* it." She paused for emphasis. "And there's a *big* difference between these two states of mind!"

She put them into small groups and gave this instruction: "Talk first about *your* experience of each mindset, then share your observations of your sales team—how *they* behave when they are above or below this line." The conversation continued for a long time. There were lots of examples of how mindset affected behavior, both for managers and for sales agents. Grace let the discussion run its course, then took the group to the next level.

"Let me share something with you that we won't share with your agents when we teach them about Above-the-Line and Below-the-Line attitudes. They don't need this information to sell well, but you will find it helpful in your work as a leadership team, and it will also sharpen your management of the people who report to you."

Grace created a diagram on the flipchart as she continued to talk (see Figure 7.1).[xix] "There are actually *different* states of mind that we slip into during the day, depending on what happens to us. There's an entire *spectrum* of mindset, from very high to very low."

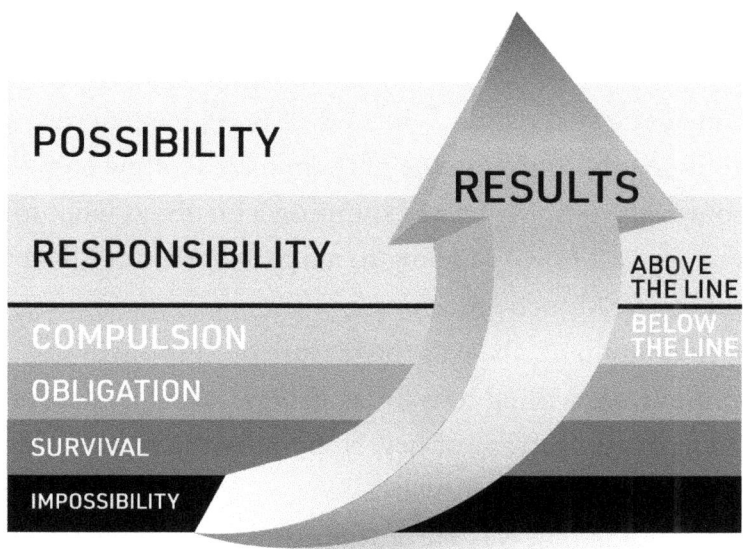

POSSIBILITY

RESULTS

RESPONSIBILITY

ABOVE
THE LINE

BELOW
THE LINE

COMPULSION

OBLIGATION

SURVIVAL

IMPOSSIBILITY

Figure 7.1 The Attitude Spectrum

The group took their time exploring the six different levels of attitude. They remembered moments when they were so *up* that nothing could get in their way. No matter the obstacle, the challenge, or the issue, they could always think of *other possibilities*—there was always a way over, under, around, or through whatever they were facing. Their creativity was a match for any problem, and their level of job satisfaction increased with the level of challenge. "When I am in that state of mind," said Sarah, the founder and CEO, "I'm fearless, unstoppable!" Others agreed.

The attitude just below Possibility—still above the line, just not as *high* a state of mind—resonated with Colette, the most experienced sales manager in the group. She was a close friend of Sarah's and a key player in the company from its earliest days. "I've just taken on the job of managing our newest sales team, in our newest region," she said. "My eight agents are very different people, and a couple of them haven't done so well in their previous jobs. My head's spinning a bit about what to do, I don't know yet how I'm going to make it work, but I'll have it figured out by Monday morning."

At that moment, she was the picture of Responsibility. She was committed, willing to try new things, and fully accepting of the challenge in front of her. Nobody in the room doubted she would find her way forward.

The attitude that was hardest for the group to identify was the first mindset below the line. "This is always the most difficult state of mind for executives and managers to spot, Grace said. "Here's what I remember when I have that nagging sensation that something's wrong. Compulsion *feels* like Responsibility—like I'm strong, moving forward, in control. And, frankly, in many sales organizations, Compulsion *passes* for peak performance. Compared to the three states below it, it looks great, and you *do* get results. In this state of mind, people work harder, keep pressing, and don't give up—no matter how they feel or what happens."

"They also burn out, blow up, and drive the rest of us crazy!"

"They also burn out, blow up, and drive the rest of us crazy!" said James, a sales manager who had watched a lot of agents come and go. The group laughed in agreement. They shared a few stories of how people they worked with or managed had gotten caught in Compulsion. In response to the trainer's prompts, they described the behavior of salespeople and sales managers caught in this state of mind—its driven-ness, aggressiveness, intolerance, and inflexibility. And they also described its impact on customers and the rest of the sales team.

Sarah spoke up. "This is my second start-up," she said, "and I completely failed the first time." She paused before continuing. "The company survived, barely. But I had to quit, and that was a tough thing to do. I had reached a point where I couldn't *stop* working. Morning, noon, and night, I was neglecting my family. I had no life other than the business, and I had to pull back or lose people close to me." She looked directly at the group. "I will *not* repeat that mistake here, and I don't want you to do it either. Believe me; it won't help us fulfill our mission. I've been there, and it sneaks up on you."

The descent into the next three levels of mindset was easier to see. The group shared several experiences of falling into Obligation, describing it as "running out of gas" after a period of compulsive activity. "That's what happened to my senior sales agent," said one manager. "He was always on time to work, but he stopped arriving early. He turned in his timesheets and reports, but as the weeks went by, they looked more and more alike. He did what was expected, but that was it."

The discussion of the Survival state of mind invited even more honesty. The group talked about the anxiety, and at times the panic, they and their teams felt at the end of most quarters. "Last year," Tanawat shared, "as Q3 was closing, I hardly slept. I kept doing everything I could think of to get my team across the finish line, and, looking back, some of those things were really stupid. They created even *more* problems for me to fix." He looked at the group. "You know what happened. My team's performance kept all of us from earning a bonus, and we lost two good salespeople who got completely frustrated and quit."

He pointed to the lowest mindset in the attitude spectrum diagram in his workbook. "That's where I spent most of Q4… in Impossibility." He turned to Sarah and nodded slightly. "I'm sorry, I knew it was my attitude, but I didn't know what to do about it. I just couldn't get over it."

The CEO reached out her hand and said, "We've all been there. Consider this a new start for all of us."

Grace pointed at the diagram and asked a final question. "What does the upward arrow indicate?" In spite of the word "Results" written in the arrowhead, it took a while for the group to make the connection between attitude and the ability to succeed in selling, managing, and leading. Once they got the point, however, it led to 20 minutes of spirited discussion.

The connection between attitude and results is one of the most fascinating contributions of transformative learning to sales performance. The teacher we spoke of earlier, who diagrammed a human being as a collection of I's, described this process as the development of an *Observing I*—an active, conscious *awareness* of what the rest of our mental machinery is doing.

Step one is to watch your state of mind as it slides up and down the Attitude Spectrum during the day. Step two is being patient with yourself—accepting your frustration and embarrassment about being Below-the-Line.

Once you *know* you're Below-the-Line, there's only one sensible step to take: *stop* what you're doing and *return* to a more productive state of mind. Maggie Appleton of Educate! looked back on the training with her senior team: "We were completely surprised at how Below-the-Line we were—no wonder we couldn't address the blocks that were in our way. Learning to shift our attitude made a huge difference to our leadership."[9]

Again, the key question is, "Yes, but how?" Years ago, we found a brilliant, effective, and fast-acting answer to this question: a simple practice called Split Attention. Thousands of people, representing a great diversity of experience, education, and culture, have learned to integrate this practice into their daily life and work.

SPLIT ATTENTION

Split Attention is a transformational practice that has connections to both traditional spiritual training and modern neuroscience,[xx] which has documented the brain's ability to develop new neural pathways: to *rewire* itself and make new behavior possible.[xxi] Split Attention's great advantage is that you don't have to stop working in order to use it to shift your state of mind. You do it *while* you work (see Figure 7.2).

---

9   Educate! tackles the problem of youth unemployment in Africa by developing educational solutions.

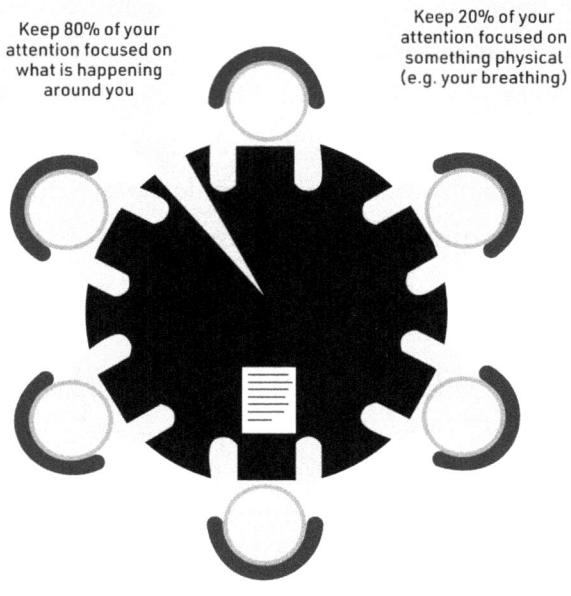

Keep 80% of your attention focused on what is happening around you

Keep 20% of your attention focused on something physical (e.g. your breathing)

Figure 7.2 Split Attention

There's a video on our website that will guide you through the technique. Sometimes, people can learn this skill by reading about it, so here is an explanation:

Keep the majority of your attention on whoever you're with or whatever you're doing. At the same time, *become aware of* something physical, something you can *feel*. You can pick *any* physical sensation. We have found two that work most often for the people we train: the movement of their stomachs while they breathe or touching two fingers to a thumb.

For example, if you're listening to a customer or a colleague, *continue* to listen *while* you feel your stomach push out as you inhale and pull back in as you exhale. You can try it now while you're reading these words. Read this paragraph again slowly. As you read, *feel* your stomach expand and contract as you breathe. See if you can do this for an entire breath while you keep reading.

Try it again, rereading the paragraph as you *feel* your first two fingers touching your thumb.

Go ahead. Read other paragraphs, alternating feeling your stomach movement with feeling the touch of your fingers.

Which sensation is easier to pay attention to as you read—your stomach moving with your breath or the touch of your fingers and thumb? You may find, as we do, that *breathing* is easier to focus on when you're listening, and *touching* is easier when you're speaking. Experiment. Find what works best for *you*.

You'll probably find that you can only stay aware of splitting your attention for 15 or 20 seconds at a time. You drift away from it until the next time you remember to split your attention. So, practicing this technique is a humbling experience. Don't try to *do it all the time;* instead, *return to it* as often as you can. When people practice Split Attention eight to ten times a day, they spend a lot more time Above-the-Line, and they produce far greater results.

It's simple to do, but it's hard to *remember* to do it. This fact, however, makes it ideal for people who work in teams. When somebody's attitude is *down*, he or she is often the last to know. Colleagues can help each other notice when Split Attention is needed.

Our clients often put *this* part of the training to work immediately. Within a couple of weeks, sales managers report that "Are you Above- or Below-the-Line?" has become a common and helpful question. And "Let's split our attention together and get back Above-the-Line" has become a critical part of the conversations between managers and the people who depend on their support. Erica Mackey said, "It is actually rather amazing how Split Attention frees up the *natural brilliance* in our providers. When they wake up from autopilot, they *know* what to do next."

We have found that awareness of the Attitude Spectrum and using Split Attention are quite possibly the most important things we've ever learned about transforming human performance. Everything else follows.

GETTING HIGH(ER)

Once you start practicing Split Attention with some regularity, you can use it to *accelerate* a skill we discussed earlier: uncovering your *Deep Desire* and finding a purpose and motivation that can fuel your highest performance.

It's easy to do.

Split your attention for a few moments. Then, focus on something you want, and use the phrases "I want…and

I want that because I want…"

Stick with it. Keep returning to splitting your attention while you write. You will find that it raises your attitude quickly, clarifies your thinking, and develops a resolve that takes you forward.

Not bad for an investment of three to five minutes.

When you get good at this, you can even do it in your head *while* you work. For example, let's say you're in the middle of a conversation that turns difficult. You notice yourself slip Below-the-Line. You ask the other person a question, and, while they're beginning to respond, you split your attention and mentally complete a sentence like: *What I want right now is…* And then extend it with a thought about: *And I want that because what I'm after is …* When you get good at this, you can elevate your attitude in seconds.

When we developed the use of Split Attention in our work, we were a bit hesitant to introduce it to the sales-people in emerging markets. Was it too sophisticated a tool? Would it just be too weird? Within minutes of teaching this in Cambodia, we had our answer. Immediately a new sales agent raised his hand and said, "Ah, I've been doing this since I was a child. I just didn't know to do it at work!" So much for our (Western) ignorance and arrogance. Lisa Mikkelsen said, "Split Attention is basic mindfulness. You can apply it to any stressful situation. It's a *tremendous* skill for anyone to learn."

Now, let's take a look at how to use Split Attention *and* have a conversation with customers and colleagues that can keep you Above-the-Line, lift the other person's attitude, and result in committed action that moves things forward.

CHAPTER 8

GENERATE COMPELLING CONVERSATIONS

Executive Summary

The *itch to pitch* is difficult to overcome, not just for sales agents but also for their managers and everyone in the company. Managers often turn into "answer machines" who simply talk too much and listen too little.

Spend half of a conversation listening, and you'll discover problems that customers or team members need to solve. And, when you help people think more deeply and clearly, they begin solving their own problems: your salespeople change their behavior, and their customers commit to the decisions they make.

You can trust the transformational framework of the CLEAR™ conversation to develop your ability to stay Above-the-Line as you engage with others. When you give up "pitching" in all its forms—trying to maneuver people into doing what you want them to do—you'll manage more effectively and lead with greater authority. Traditional sales training is filled with the "Three Ts"—tips, tricks, and techniques: how to pitch, how and when to ask the right questions, how to overcome objections, and, of course, how to close the sale. Such training reduces selling to a matter of technique. And, when the context of this content—the fundamental assumption that drives it—is that selling is convincing customers to buy stuff, then technique easily slides into manipulation.

Conducting genuinely non-manipulative conversations is a key *competence* for DQ sellers and their managers. Competence is the "C" in the R=A+C+E™ formula (see Figure 2.1): how to structure a conversation that *requires* people to remain Above-the-Line and results in consciously chosen actions that people are committed to taking. This skill is the ability to engage in a CLEAR™, conversation. Salespeople use it to raise the DQ of their customers, and sales managers use it to develop their teams.

Nearly always, having a CLEAR™ conversation requires a *significant* change of behavior on the part of the person leading it. Primarily, they have to talk a lot less and listen a lot more. And this is usually a challenge for people in sales—especially when they get anxious, especially when the pressure is on.

Most sales managers are aware of this problem. Over and over again, they watch their team members fail to listen long enough to learn the breadth and depth of the problems their customers face. When a customer need appears, agents often stop listening to go for the sale. This actually decreases their chance of making the sale and misses the opportunity for a larger one. Agents just don't listen very well when they think their job is to talk.

THE ITCH TO PITCH

Given the context surrounding sales, virtually everybody expects your salespeople to start pitching.

Your *leaders* expect it. Even people who aren't in sales—finance, tech, HR—think sales agents should greet customers with a *value proposition*. "Sales training" is mostly about the features, benefits, and advantages of the company's goods and services. We remember a client who put their new agents through a week-long sales training: thirty-eight hours of product and technical instruction and two hours of technique. The meta-message in such trainings is not *Show up and listen*; it's *Go forth and pitch*.

Your *customers* expect it. They're used to "being sold." They'll often ignore your agent's questions about their needs and *demand* that the agents pitch them instead: *What are you selling? How does it work? How much does it cost?*

Your *salespeople* expect it. They think their credibility and trustworthiness come from *explaining* what they're selling and demonstrating its superiority. They actually believe that the more knowledgeable and persuasive they are about the product, the greater their chances of making the sale.

But what if everyone realized that demonstrating product knowledge and pitching *doesn't* really establish a salesperson's credibility or generate a customer's trust? What if your sales agents recognized that arriving with a convincing case makes them *look like everybody else who comes knocking on the door?* What if they awakened to the fact that *nobody* really finds this process helpful or enjoyable—not the customer, not even themselves?

> What if demonstrating product knowledge and pitching *doesn't* really establish a salesperson's credibility or generate a customer's trust?

So *how* does a consumer-facing salesperson do something *different,* something that actually *leads* customers to the *discoveries* that enable them to buy wisely, be confident in their decision, and commit to following through by using the product, making their loan payments, and referring their friends?

And how do sales *managers* stop "pitching" the agents they manage? How do they stop giving the same advice over and over again, telling their people what to do and trying to motivate them to do it? How do they genuinely *empower* their sales teams to think deeply, solve problems, and develop confidence? How do they stop the autopilot behavior of oscillating between micromanaging their direct reports or leaving them on their own?

Let's return to the training room to learn how to do this. And this time, let's stand in the trainer's shoes.

CREATING COMMITTED ACTION

Transformational training has its unique demands. It's not straightforward, and it doesn't "follow the manual." You have to lead people at a pace that works for them—managers first and then the sales agents. You've got to make three things happen: create a fresh, often surprising *experience*; get them to share that experience with their colleagues; and recognize that, while they were doing these two things, they've made a simple, natural, and welcome change in their behavior.

Transformational trainers learn that you can't do this by following specific steps. You have to keep splitting your attention, stay Above-the-Line, and trust that human beings *want* to wake up from autopilot, start thinking for themselves, and enjoy being at their best.

Let's join one of these trainers—we'll call him Francisco—who's working with the CEO and the sales leadership team of a Brazilian company that provides safe access to clean water for the rural poor. It's the third day of training, and the group has just finished discussing the challenges of helping sales agents adopt a different mindset about selling and change their selling behavior.

Francisco introduces the next exercise with a direct question: "May I ask you to do a simple exercise without explaining why we're doing it?" The group is eager, and Francisco asks everyone to choose a partner with whom they're willing to have a serious conversation.

Everyone's a bit nervous, but they choose a colleague and move their chairs closer together. Francisco introduces the exercise. "To make this a real conversation and not another role play," he says, "you're going to talk about real challenges that you and your colleagues are facing as you manage the work of your sales teams. And you're going to see if you can listen carefully enough that you can *accurately play back* to them what they say. You may find you're really good at this. You may find that it's a lot harder than it looks."

Francisco asks for a volunteer, and Adriana joins him at the front of the room. Francisco draws a vertical line on a flip chart page, dividing the page into two sections (see Figure 8.1).

Figure 8.1 Precision Listening

He says to the group, "Watch what I do and what I *don't* do." He turns to Adriana and invites her to start talking about her challenge.

"Well," Adriana begins, "I can't figure out what Ernesto, one of my more experienced sales agents, is doing wrong. A high percentage of his customers don't make their payments after they've signed contracts. I spend a lot of time talking to him about this problem, and he's genuinely concerned. I even took three hours out of my day to observe him last week, and I still don't understand his problem. He explains the system well, and customers seem really excited when they sign up." Adriana takes a deep breath and shakes her head.

Francisco writes a few words and a symbol in the left column of the flip chart page: "hi %," "no paym," "watched," "explain," "excited," "don't know why." He circles "watched" and "explain," and he draws arrows from those words to the right-hand column, where he puts question marks. He turns to Adriana and says, "So, a high percentage of Ernesto's customers aren't making their payments. You've spoken to him; he's concerned; and you've even observed him at work. He explains things well, and his customers are excited. And you're frustrated."

Francisco doesn't say anything else. He looks at Adriana and waits for her to continue.

"Do I just keep going?" Adriana asks. Francisco just smiles, the group laughs nervously, and Adriana takes a breath. Then she carries on, speaking more deliberately as she thinks out loud. "Given what we've learned here," she says, "I'm wondering if he's explaining things *too* well—if he's just talking too much..."

She thinks a bit longer and nods her head. "You know, he's actually *talking them into* buying rather than helping them discover why they need our program. He *convinces* them to sign, but they don't really commit."

As Adriana continues, Francisco makes a few more notes and then says, "You're beginning to wonder if Ernesto's ability to explain things is the problem. He's talking customers into buying, and they're not really committed to what they're signing up for."

Adriana immediately responds: "Yes, exactly. Come to think of it, he *does* talk too much. He's so excited about what we're offering, and he has so much information about the product that—" she pauses for a moment and then finishes with, "he just needs to shut up more!" That draws a lot of laughter.

"And," she says, "I also think it's true that he gets nervous. And the more nervous he gets, the more he keeps talking. I don't know how to get him to stop."

Francisco keeps taking notes on both the left and right sides of the vertical line, pausing every minute or so to play back to Adriana what she says. Within a few minutes, she has an idea: "I remember when you taught us Split Attention two days ago. I'm thinking it could really help Ernesto calm down."

Francisco stops the conversation at this point. Then he asks the group, "What did you see me doing with Adriana?"

It takes a moment for everyone to pull their attention away from Adriana and put it onto Francisco's question. Selena observes that Francisco had faithfully repeated back to Adriana the main points of what she was saying, sometimes even using her exact words. João notices that Francisco used his notes to remember what Adriana had said. Paulo points out that

Francisco hadn't referred to any of his notes on the *right* side of the line.

Francisco is itching to make some points, but he stays disciplined about listening for *their* insights before sharing his own. "What did I *not* do?" *he asks.*

Several people respond. "You didn't ask any questions." "You didn't offer any suggestions." "You didn't steer the conversation in one direction or another—you just stayed quiet. *How do you do that?" Good-natured laughter.*

Francisco keeps the conversation on track. "We call this Precision Listening," he says. "And here's an important question: what *happened* to Adriana when I *didn't* ask any questions, make any suggestions, or guide her in any particular direction?"

> "What *happened* to Adriana when I *didn't* ask any questions, make any suggestions, or guide her in any particular direction?"

Adriana speaks first. "I started solving my own problem!" *This* is a revelation. Francisco wonders if the three sales managers are thinking more deeply about how to help their direct reports solve problems, and he makes a mental note to bring it up later if they don't mention it first.

Francisco decides it is time for the group to stop talking and start practicing. He directs them to workbook pages that are blank except for a vertical line. "Make your notes about what your *colleague* says on the left side of the line," he instructs. "As you think of things *you* want to ask or say, put those notes on the *right* side of the line. Every minute or so, play back what *they* said, but keep your *own* thoughts and questions to yourself."

Francisco coaches each pair as they work. He's excited when someone listens well, and he manages his frustration when they don't. He gives short, helpful directions to the person who is doing the listening and keeps them in conversation.

As he moves from pair to pair, people respond quickly to his interventions, and he's pleased with the quality of his coaching. Then, he runs into Mateus. He watches Mateus tap his pen on his paper while his partner talks. Mateus isn't taking notes, and when his partner pauses—actually giving him time to play back—Mateus just nods for her to continue.

"You're not playing back what Selena is saying?" Francisco asks. "*She* knows I'm listening," he snaps. "I don't get why we're doing this anyway. This would never work in the real world!" Francisco starts to explain the purpose of the exercise before he realizes his attitude has dropped Below-the-Line. Mateus is being rude, and he doesn't like it.

Francisco takes a breath and splits his attention. His irritation fades, and he says, "Mateus, I'm wasting your practice time by repeating what I've already said. I know this seems strange, and I know you're not the only one with that question. I'll make you a deal. You just keep practicing, and I'll answer your question when we get the group back together. Okay?" Mateus agrees, and Francisco steps away.

After a few more minutes, Francisco gathers the group together. The debrief is enthusiastic and informative.

"I've never had anyone just listen while I talked. It gave me time to realize what I really thought," says Lucas, one of the sales managers.

"My colleague really *did* know what to do," offers Patricia. "I'm so used to thinking I have to solve everybody's problems— I could hardly keep my mouth shut and just listen!" There are some knowing smiles around the room.

"I just had a revelation," says Gabriela, a new hire. "The more João listened to me—" she nods at her colleague, who is sitting to her left, "the more I kept talking. He was great. He gave me room to think, take my time, and find my words. I actually shared more than I thought I would." She pauses a moment. "It's strange, but even though I have no idea what he's thinking about what I said, I feel comfortable around him."

This last comment gets the group thinking about the conversations their agents have with customers. What if agents listened like this, especially when customers were talking about the difficulties of accessing clean water and what life was like without it? What impact might *that* have on the sales conversation?

Adriana raises her hand. "I think I see what I've been doing wrong with Ernesto. I'm talking instead of listening and giving him advice instead of just playing back what he says. I'm not giving him the chance to solve his own problem."

The group continues to talk for another few minutes about the effects of listening deeply and well. Francisco starts to introduce the next step, but he notices Mateus looking at him, and he remembers his promise.

"Before we go on," he says, "Mateus raised a question that I'm thinking many of you have. How many of you are thinking that you'd never behave like this in a real conversation?" Half the group raises their hands. Mateus smiles.

"What's the part of it that you don't feel comfortable doing? What seems different or strange?"

It takes a few minutes, and two difficulties emerge. For some, it is the playback itself. "I don't want to sound like a parrot," Mateus says. "Me too," adds Gabriela, "but I especially don't want to sit there in silence, watching them struggle to figure out what to say next."

Francisco asks Adriana a question: "When I was repeating what you said, did I sound like a parrot?" Some laughter around the room, but also some glances of real interest.

Adriana thinks before she responds. "There were a couple of times when I realized you were using my exact words...but actually, it just made me think more deeply about what I really meant." She pauses a moment. "And it was clear that you were listening carefully to what I was saying."

Francisco turns to the group, "You'll get better at doing this, and you'll only sound like a parrot if you're preoccupied with doing it 'right.' Instead, just focus on accurately hearing the other person and playing back enough of what they've said to make sure they know you've heard them. You'll find that a lot of interesting things happen.

"It's helpful to leave a *bit* of silence—people need room to think."

"And about the silence—" he adds, "in selling *and* in sales management conversations, it's helpful to leave a *bit* of silence—people need room to think. But you don't want to let the silence get long and awkward. Just be careful not to fill it with things that *take the conversation away* from the other person—like introducing another subject or asking a question that pulls them in a new direction."

Francisco continues: "Here's how to make the silence helpful instead of awkward. Look at the left-hand side of your notes, find something that you're curious about, and then just say, 'Tell me more about this.'"

This simple idea strikes a chord with the sales managers. It's not manipulative or controlling, and it provides a way to keep the other person moving forward, digging deeper, investing more in the conversation.

The discussion starts to slow down, and just as Francisco is wondering if it's time to move forward, Daniela raises her hand.

"I've just realized something," she says. "By following my colleague's lead, I learned things I wouldn't have thought to ask. And it gave me time to develop a few ideas that might be of help."

"Yes, that's the next step," Francisco says. "Look at your notes on the right-hand side of the page. You'll probably find that some of those things are no longer necessary to mention. And some are *very* necessary. You may have questions. You may have guidance. You may think something they are planning to do is brilliant or a huge mistake.

"Say what you think. See what happens. *They* have the responsibility of deciding what to do. What they need from *you* is your honest and direct opinion before they make that decision."

The pairs launch into spirited conversation. Francisco doesn't coach them this time. He watches them work and feels energy and vitality fill the room.

When this part of the exercise is complete, he gives a final instruction. "You've listened deeply and without interruption as your colleagues explored their challenges. You've offered your own honest opinions about what they're facing. What's the obvious next step? What's going to make this conversation worth the time you've both invested?"

Adriana smiles and says, "Ask them what they're going to *do* about it!"

"Exactly," says Francisco. "And here's a way to do it that gets things moving: don't ask for a plan; ask for a Very Next Step (VNS)." [xxii] This suggestion leads to a discussion of the paralyzing habit of trying to develop elaborate plans before taking action. It feels faster and freer to identify the *very* next thing to do, go do it, and *then* figure out what to do next. It only takes a few minutes for each pair of colleagues to choose a VNS.

Francisco then says, "There's a final step to take. Ask your colleague if there's *anything* that could get in the way of taking their very next step."

After a short discussion, five people make adjustments to their VNS. This proves the point. It's easy to fall back into autopilot and overlook what's standing in your way. And it's easy to avoid this if someone asks you to take a closer look. Simple and helpful.

Francisco introduces the conversational framework they just experienced. "It's called CLEAR™," he says, "and I use it to guide *every* conversation I have, whether I'm selling to a customer, managing my team, working with a colleague, dealing with a customer complaint, or meeting one-on-one with my own manager."

The group spends the next half hour discussing the finer points of the model and how it might change the conversations they have with their team members.

Then, Adriana raises an important point. "My sales agents—and especially Ernesto—need to learn how to do this with customers. Do I have to take them through everything we just did?"

"Take a close look at the Sight Seller," Francisco says. He waits for the group to start flipping through the sales aid. "As agents use the Sight Seller to guide customers through the four stages of the conversation—Problem, Cost, Solution, Value—what do you see happening?"

It takes a few minutes, but Adriana figures it out first. "It's all based on CLEAR™," she says. "It helps the agent alternate between listening carefully to the client and educating them as needed. It gives time for the customer to understand, and it asks for their commitment. I see how it works!" Francisco puts them into small groups to discuss her insight.[10]

> **"It's all based on CLEAR™!"**

Here is the CLEAR™ framework, the model for which is contained in Figure 8.2.

- **Connect:** People buy from people they like and trust. That's why *establishing rapport* is so critical to a successful

---

10 We do suggest teaching CLEAR™ to agents after they've mastered the Sight Seller or if they are engaged in any sort of extended or B2B-type sales conversations. It is a highly effective way to deal with customer objections and concerns.

conversation. It's not just happy talk; it's a skillful blend of connecting at both the professional and personal levels. In the first few minutes of a conversation, it's also important to agree on an agenda, the outcome you're after, and how much time you have to talk. These three things frame the conversation you're about to have. And, very importantly, it lets you know how much time you've got for the next step.

- **Learn:** The "L" icon in the figure is filled with a solid color. This is a reminder to spend approximately *half* of the conversation using the skill of *Precision Listening,* as illustrated in the story of Francisco's training. Whether you're selling, managing, or collaborating with colleagues, learning more about *their* thinking is the key to stimulating your *own* thinking. Take your time; follow their lead. Say, "tell me more" to help them go deeper. Refuse to control the conversation. Follow your curiosity. Learn something new so that you have something new to work with. *Split Attention is the key to doing this consistently and well. About halfway through the conversation,* move on to the next step, or you won't have enough time to create the committed action you're after.

- **Educate:** When the time for Learning has run its course, ask for permission before you move to this stage: "Is there anything else you want me to hear before I share what I've been thinking about this?" Often there will be one more thing they want you to know or understand. You'll be glad you waited until now to ask your questions and provide your input. You'll wind up saying less and having more impact. Be considerate and direct. It's their responsibility to decide what to do, but it's your responsibility to give them your best thinking. Leave a few minutes for the final two steps.

- **Ask for action:** When you've done the Learn and Educate steps as thoroughly as time permits, it is natural and easy to raise the subject of a Very Next Step. The other person needs to decide what to *do* in order to move this conversation into action. You may have suggestions about what the next step needs to be. Be sure to ask for their ideas first, but don't be shy about offering your own. The goal here is to help the other person get Above-the-Line in their attitude and make a commitment they want to keep.

- **Resolve:** This step is an *autopilot check*. In its simplest form, you ask the other person to think for a moment about what might get in the way of completing their VNS on time. They will wake up to any conflicts or potential obstacles and adjust their next step accordingly.

> The goal is to help the other person get Above-the-Line in their attitude and make a commitment they want to keep.

This simple step leads to a committed choice. Occasionally, the person you're speaking with just isn't ready to take a VNS. There's something blocking them—perhaps a customer has an objection, or a direct report is struggling with a way forward. What you need to do is cycle back through CLEAR™, returning to the "L" step to learn more about what's in their way so that you can support them to resolve it. If you need to have another conversation to do this, schedule it before you stop.

Our clients use CLEAR™ to guide their management conversations. Maggie Appleton said that this model was the greatest surprise of her training. "Now I know how to be with my senior team—the questions to ask, the way to converse with them so everyone is called to think deeply about the data in front of us and make the decisions required to lead our company forward."

 This conversational framework takes practice. You'll be surprised how quickly you get good at some steps while struggling with others. Don't sweat it. Keep practicing. It will pay off.

Now onto *execution*, where the critical role of the sales manager takes center stage.

CONNECT personally and professionally
- Make introductions and establish rapport.
- Set the agenda and timeframe.
- Save half the time for the **Learn** step.

LEARN about the situation
- Use Precision Listening and replay.
- Resist the urge to jump in—keep listening.
- Use *"Tell me more"* to open up conversation.

EDUCATE appropriately
- Get permission to share your thinking.
- Share your input boldly to set up next actions.
- Discuss the subject collaboratively.

ASK for action
- Ask questions to test interest.
- Ask for their very next step.
- Provide two alternatives if possible.

RESOLVE any blocks or concerns
- Replay the block, use S/A, and ask for others.
- Use Precision Listening for each block.
- Resolve the biggest block and get the VNS.

Figure 8.2 CLEAR Conversation

CHAPTER 9

BUILD YOUR PEOPLE

Executive Summary

Execution is a virtuous loop of three fundamental activities: salespeople *aim* themselves wisely, work in a state of Flow, and continue to *build* their capacity to play their part in the development of your business.

Transformation requires leadership, and this is the job of the sales manager. It requires support from above and a **structure** of engagement between manager and team that empowers your sales agents to **execute** your selling system.

Your sales managers create the conditions for *execution* to flourish. Special Numbers provide key data. A transformed sales meeting and three distinct types of one-to-one conversations create a learning environment that generates outstanding sales results.

You don't build a business—you build people—
and people build the business.[xxiii]

Everyone agrees that sales managers are responsible for the performance of their teams. What's far less clear is exactly *what* sales managers are supposed to do to make this performance happen. Solving this puzzle requires a deep understanding of *execution*, the "E" in R=A+C+E™ (see Figure 2.1). And in both emerging and developed markets, the sad truth is that good sales management is surprisingly difficult to find.

"When I tried to turn selling over to our new sales managers and their teams," said Anushka Ratnayake, "I found that they simply missed out on sales they could have made. We reached a point in our growth where we needed our sales managers to be as good at coaching as they were at selling—and that's a hard transition."

A social entrepreneur, who wanted to remain anonymous, said, "We decided to hire all our sales managers from outside the company. I think we thought that none of our own people knew how to do the job and that perhaps someone 'out there' did. Well, they *didn't* know, and we paid a big price for bringing them in."

This last comment reveals something important. Sales management—the art and the science of developing and sustaining an effective sales team—is often *more* of a black box than selling is. You can see this clearly when you look at how most sales managers are "trained" for their role. Either they are parachuted into the company because they were a sales manager at another company, or they are promoted from within according to a process wryly described by one of our commercial clients. "On Friday at 6 p.m., I was the company's number one seller," he said. "On Monday morning at 8 a.m., I was the newest sales manager. I must have missed the management training over the weekend."

As new sales managers painfully learn, *managing* requires a different set of skills than *selling*. Yes, it helps to have sold—in fact, it's *essential*. But, especially for managers who want to develop a high performing team, there are additional skills that must be mastered.

Use the categories of R=A+C+E™ as lenses to look at both roles. It's pretty clear that sales agents *and* their managers need to get really good at focusing on the right *results* (aiming), managing their *attitude* (using Split Attention to stay Above-the-Line), and conducting *competent* conversations (using CLEAR™ to get to committed action).

When it comes to *execution*, however, we see the unique and critical role that sales managers play—not only in the *development* of the team but especially in creating the conditions for that team to *keep* learning and developing. We have learned the hard way—not only with our own clients but in our own business—that unless you have sales managers who know how to *build* their people by paying impeccable and disciplined attention to the right details, a sales team simply can't keep performing at their best.

Lindsay Stradley of Sanergy said, "Our biggest lever to improving our sales performance wasn't technical training; it was learning to manage

> "When sales managers realized that *it was their job* to continually develop their team members, our sales grew like never before."

our *people*."[11] Eduardo Bontempo told us: "It was training our sales *managers* that created a sustainable sales force. When they realized that *it was their job* to continually develop their team members, our sales grew like never before."

How do sales managers create the conditions for this continuous development to happen?

THE EXECUTION CYCLE

From a transformational point of view, effective sales managers ensure that their agents keep repeating a specific *cycle* of activities that *invite and require* their team members to keep choosing to develop into high performers because they really want to.

The Execution Cycle has three phases, each of which prepares you for the next (see Figure 9.1). *Aiming* your brain at the results you seek launches you into activity that, when done with an Above-the-Line state of mind, results in a high level of naturally brilliant performance that has been called "Flow." [xxiv] To ensure your aim stays true and to remain in Flow, you need consistent and effective periods of time when you step back from activity, reflect on what's happened, and learn from it. This is the Build phase, the development opportunity that legendary sales managers live for. One of our commercial clients, a terrific sales manager, often said, "I don't manage people, I *develop* them."

---

11   Sanergy operates in Kenya, offering products and services that provide a safe and effective solution to the problems of urban sanitation.

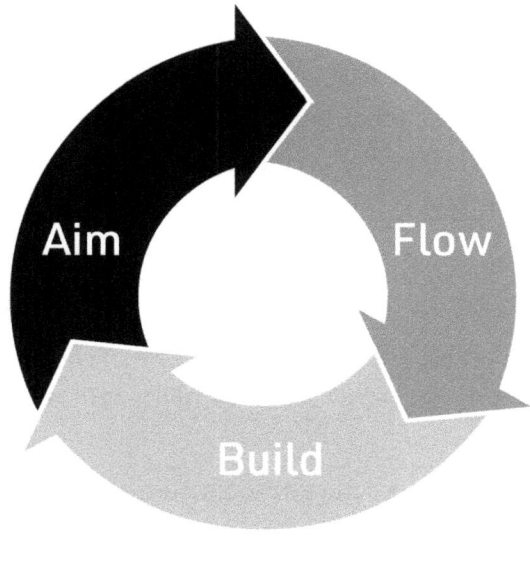

Figure 9.1 The Execution Cycle

It follows, then, that if you're going to transform your sales force, you *first* have to transform your sales managers. This requires—from everyone involved—discipline, curiosity, and a willingness to learn.

What does that look like in a social enterprise that depends on effective B2C selling to achieve impact?

A WEEK IN THE LIFE OF A SALES MANAGER

Imagine you're a sales manager with a team of seven agents. The CEO has entrusted to you the responsibility for implementing the company's new DQ Selling system.

When you left the manager's training three weeks ago, you knew that your very next step was to *practice* the skills you were introduced to. You're getting the hang of it. Your awareness of your attitude is growing each week, and you are using Split Attention more frequently during the day. You're aiming yourself thoughtfully on a weekly and daily basis, and you've survived your initial clumsiness with CLEAR™ conversations. You understand the specifics of your new selling system: the four steps your customers must take to raise their DQ, the Sight Seller that your agents use to help them do this, and the simple tracking system your agents use to plan, record, and analyze their selling activity.

Two weeks ago, you and your team completed the sales training. The team is enthusiastic, and you're ready for the second full week of implementing what you've learned. You've got a plan, a structure to follow. You know you can't do it all perfectly, but you're going to give it your best. You remember a quote from your training: "Be careful of the illusion that a quick win is just around the corner. Remember, it's *gradual* change."[12]

"Be careful of the illusion that a quick win is just around the corner. Remember, it's *gradual* change."

You've taken a hard look at the management behaviors you want to change. You're going to focus on: inputs and not just outputs, developing your team members instead of driving them, preparing for meetings instead of "winging" it, and requiring your team to work the new DQ Selling system with rigor and discipline.

---

12   From Maggie Appleton.

You've planned your week. You've got a carefully constructed series of activities designed to create the conditions in which your team members can keep *building* their sales capability. You've scheduled a sales meeting every morning for the next month to get the right behaviors in place; then, you'll gradually back it off to once or twice a week. You've got the right number of one-to-one phone calls and meetings scheduled with each member of your team. You've received their Aim Plans for the week ahead, and you've noted a few things to watch out for.[13] You've dumped your old team meeting format—that exercise in boredom and repetition—and you're ready for something new.

Monday

You arrive an hour early to plan your sales meeting. You review the Special Numbers from last week and the notes from your one-to-one Personal Conferences.[14] You make a list of the "wins" that your team members had last week: their sales (the output) and their activities and practices (the inputs). You have already decided that the most important practice to refresh for everyone is the ability to stay Above-the-Line, and you've asked Margarita—who's doing this well—to prepare a 15-minute exercise for the group. You go to the meeting room early and make sure it's set exactly as you want it.

You welcome people warmly as they arrive. You start the meeting on time by introducing the agenda, and then you

---

13   More about Aim Plans below.

14   See Personal Conferences below.

mention by name each person who contributed something significant the previous week: growth in the number of doors knocked on, presentations given, and personal victories over anxiety, hesitancy, and stepping up to challenges. Then you acknowledge the particular sales results that were especially noteworthy.

Margarita takes the group through her exercise on staying Above-the-Line. She stumbles a little at one point, but you let her recover on her own. She finishes strong and receives a round of applause from her colleagues. You share information that pertains to everybody on the team: two company announcements and a product update.

You then give everyone some time to develop their Aim Plan for the week, structuring it around their Special Numbers. Then they quickly develop today's plan, and you give enough time for everyone—including yourself—to declare their aim for the day. You help them coordinate their schedules, eliminating overlaps and unproductive activity. As they share, you make your final decision about who you will observe today.

You make sure that each person is scheduled for a Check-In phone call near the end of the day and that each person knows when their one-to-one Personal Conference is scheduled with you for later in the week. It's a lively conversation, and you're pleased to see several instances of cooperative activity that wouldn't have happened without this meeting.

When everyone has shared their plans, you ask a direct question: "What might get in the way of you fulfilling your plan for today?" The next few minutes are refreshing and constructive.

There's no complaining, but there *is* honest discussion about anticipated difficulties. You make sure that each difficulty is addressed, and you encourage the mutual support required for everyone to accomplish their aims for the day. When you notice individual issues arise, you remind yourself to "praise in public and correct in private." You make a note to raise these issues during your individual Check-In calls.

You finish the meeting on time, get on your motorbike, and head to the field with your team. Upon arriving, you accompany Rafael as he calls on customers. He's newer to the company, and although he's not yet a top seller, he's a quick learner and worth this investment of your time.

As you walk together toward the first home he will visit, you ask if he would like to review any section of the Sight Seller. He says he's ready. You arrive at the customer's house, and, after being introduced, you stay quiet as Rafael walks his customer through the sales conversation. You notice some mistakes: he rushes through the introduction, and he doesn't really make use of his selfie photos with the neighbors he sold to earlier.

You wish he had taken you up on your offer of a rehearsal, and you're *really* tempted to jump in and help him out. But you don't. You use Split Attention to stay calm and quiet, and you let him stay in the lead. He surprises you by smoothly returning to sharing the neighbor photos. He even flips backward in the Sight Seller to do it. It's not a perfect presentation, but it's effective. And you note that he figured out how to do it himself.

The customer doesn't buy, saying that she needs her husband to be a part of the decision. Rafael addresses the block by using the CLEAR™ framework, but it still results in no decision. You can tell that he's disappointed, but he hides it well and makes an appointment for a return visit in the afternoon when the husband will be there.

You leave the house together, and you take a few minutes to review the conversation he just conducted. You spotted four mistakes, but you choose the one that's the most important one for him to fix first. You take him through a quick CLEAR™ conversation in which he acknowledges his mistake, develops a couple of ideas on how to correct it, hears your input, and then commits to what he will do in the sales conversation at the next house.

An hour and a half pass quickly. You notice that Rafael proudly tracks the results of each conversation on his Special Numbers worksheet. He uses those numbers to ask your advice on how he's doing, and you're pleased with his progress. Even more importantly, *he's* pleased with what he's doing.

You manage to work with another member of your team before lunch. You head back to the office for two essential start-of-the-week management meetings. The late afternoon is spent checking in with each of your team members, recording their Special Numbers for the day, having quick discussions about tactics, and making sure they're sticking to a tight territory plan, working systematically through their area to see everyone who lives there.

You finish the day on a high.

Tuesday and Wednesday

You start both days with the sales team meeting. At one meeting, you ask Rosa to share how she politely resisted talking with a customer about price until that page appeared near the end of the Sight Seller. At the other, you give Juan five minutes to explain how he plans his daily route; he has increased his number of presentations per day by 35% in just the first week following his training, and he makes several suggestions that are received well by the team. At both meetings, you acknowledge specific achievements in inputs and outputs, and you ensure that each person forms an Aim Plan for the day. These meetings are finding their rhythm.

You spend the mornings coaching individual team members as they work. On Wednesday, your observations are going well enough that you decide to spend the entire morning with Antonio. He's living up to his reputation as a talker, and he needs a lot of development. First, he's got to learn how to use Split Attention to calm down. Then, he needs to get a lot better at Precision Listening as he takes customers through the Sight Seller. This is very difficult for him, and you take extra time between sales conversations to help him stay Above-the-Line and practice his listening skills with you. Progress is slow, and you make a note to spend more time with him on Friday morning.

On both afternoons, you have set aside two hours for Personal Conferences with four of your team members. In each conference, you focus on their Special Numbers for the last five days. You use them to help your agents discover what they're doing well and where they need to get better. Those five numbers reveal everything.

You keep an eye on their attitude as you talk with them, helping them get back Above-the-Line when they get discouraged and supporting them to get in touch again and again with their *Deep Desire:* the *why* that motivates their work. You use the workbooks from their training to recall and practice the skills they need to master. This is the part of the job you especially enjoy, and each conversation finishes with an acknowledgment of what's been learned. Always a good sign.

On one of the afternoons, you sit down with Yolanda, one of your most experienced agents, for her once-a-month Professional Reflection: a conversation that focuses on job satisfaction, career reflection, and future planning. You're careful to stay on the subject, delegating any immediate selling concerns to the next Check-In or Personal Conference. The conversation takes several personal turns, providing helpful insight you can use to pave the way for her to become a sales manager— a dream of hers for the past six months.

You finish both days with your Check-In calls to each member of your team. You keep the calls short, and you avoid long stories— either listening to them or telling them. You keep a sharp eye on their mindset, helping them raise their attitude when necessary.

> You keep a sharp eye on their mindset, helping them raise their attitude when necessary.

Thursday and Friday

Delightfully, more of the same: a well-planned morning sales meeting, followed by coaching in the field, using afternoons for completion of all Personal Conferences and one more monthly Professional Reflection. The last thing you do before leaving the office is to have your Check-In calls, gathering everyone's Special Numbers, and quickly handling critical details. Some calls have challenging moments, but they help you stay sharp, and you're pleased with the learning your team is demonstrating.

The last half of Friday is filled with management meetings to complete the week. You're pleased that you're keeping these to a minimum and grateful that the CEO is supporting you to do that. Developing your people requires a lot of time, and you think now and then of friends who work elsewhere and complain about all the meetings that "just don't leave me any time to be with my people."

Before you leave on Friday, you set your own Aim Plan for the following week. You are learning that you cannot *force* people to transform themselves and implement DQ Selling. But you can *require* them to do the things by which they will *transform themselves* to sell in this new way.

You notice that the people who adopt these practices *want* to keep working in this way. You're also acutely aware that Raul is strongly resisting the process. You have a calm conviction that, soon, either he will quit, or you'll let him go. It won't be a surprise. There's no need for him, or you, to be miserable. You're building a high-performing team of people who find this way of working exhilarating and rewarding, and you're keeping your eyes on the prize. And he will be happier working in a less demanding environment.

You leave work on time and head for home, family, and friends.

THE KEY PRACTICES

In this imaginary "week in the life" of a sales manager, we included some of the transformational practices our customers have found invaluable. They are simple and effective. Do them consistently and masterfully, and you will build self-motivating and self-correcting teams that transform their sales performance by focusing on the DQ of their customers.

The most important practice, of course, is to keep a watchful eye on *your own* attitude, your own state of mind, as you work. Maintain an Above-the-Line mindset that allows you to access your Deep Desire and the natural brilliance that brings out your best. Have CLEAR™ conversations with colleagues and customers that lift them Above-the-Line and generate committed action.

The second most important thing is to maintain a simple *structure of engagement* with your sales agents: a set of practices and conversations that *require* them to behave in ways that create the conditions for their continued transformation and development. Here's a list of the practices you can use to build your people so they can build your business.[15]

The Sales Team Meeting
A well-designed meeting starts the day (or the week) in a way that *everyone* finds valuable: don't manage individual people in a

---

15   For more information, visit our website: WRPartnership.com

group setting—save development conversations for one-to-one meetings. Recognize specific achievements, agree on plans for the coming week, identify and remove blocks to the success of these plans, refresh skills, and pass on information everyone needs to have. Focus on the *whole* team and getting them ready to go. You can meet in person or remotely, but if you're going to work remotely, be sure to use video conferencing. It is *so* much more effective than voice only.

The Three Conversations

Highly effective sales managers have learned *not* to have the same conversation over and over again with their sales agents. They treat each team member as an individual, and they have three *distinct* kinds of interactions. In each conversation, they utilize the CLEAR™ framework and keep in mind all three elements of R=A+C+E™: attitude, competence, and execution. And they make sure each conversation is WMT—*worth my time*—for everyone involved.

- **Check-Ins** last a maximum of 10 minutes. They occur at the end of the day and more often if needed. In the final Check-In of the day, you receive the agent's report on their Special Numbers, and you log them into a central tracking system—often a spreadsheet visible to other managers and to the CEO. This gives everyone immediate visibility of what's happening. In turn, this eliminates a *lot* of "How's it going?" phone calls and emails. It's a real time saver. These short Check-In calls focus on tactics, exchanges of information, and quickly managing mindset to keep the salesperson in Flow. Done well, these calls greatly reduce interruptions, avoid delays, and address issues before they become crises.

- **Personal Conferences** occur weekly. Take a full, uninterrupted hour for this one-to-one meeting. Review the past week's Special Numbers in detail, looking for strengths to build upon and restraints to resolve. It's all there in the numbers, and helping your agents see them through your eyes will accelerate their development and increase their performance. Acknowledge what they've done well, help them learn from their mistakes, and ensure they create an Aim Plan for the following week.

- **Professional Reflections** happen monthly. In these meetings, *avoid* discussing the details of sales strategies and tactics. Instead, focus on the big picture. Have a 50,000-foot conversation about life and work. Ask about the job itself, their level of fulfillment, and personal satisfaction. Explore their career aspirations and discover what you can do to help them succeed and advance. Focus their attention on the personal and professional development they want over the next 30 days and commit to the part you can play in it. Have these conversations faithfully and well, and you will stop having surprises and difficulties when it comes time for the annual performance appraisal. You'll find the heavy lifting has already been done, and their trust in your leadership established.

Invest your time and energy into the growth of your direct reports, and you will build a team that will walk over hot coals for you.

The Right Data

All three of these transformational conversations need to be based on *reality*—things that *actually* happened or failed to happen. Everything else is *story-telling* and, to be blunt, *useless* in creating behavior change. So many management conversations wander down roads to nowhere: explanations, excuses, insights, and suggestions that change little except the level of frustration felt by everyone involved.

Building a salesperson's ability to perform requires the right data—nothing extra—and data that is accurate and timely. Most social enterprises don't gather the data they need to create behavior change in their staff. Lindsay Stradley noticed this at the senior level of her company: "We just weren't very good at making data-driven decisions. We didn't know how to collect the right data, analyze it, or use it."

Another client, who requested anonymity, had a parallel problem. "Our CEO is in love with technology. He's never found a problem a new app couldn't cure." The result was a *flood* of data that washed over sales managers on a weekly basis: little of which was actually helpful and most of which was just plain confusing.

This is where Special Numbers come in. That sales director worked with his managers to identify five numbers that would give them and their agents the information they needed to plan, track, and continuously improve their ability to sell effectively:

- Number of Presentations the agents aimed to have
- Number of Presentations (Sight Seller conversations)
- Number of Sales
- Value of Sales made
- Number of Deposits received

It took a few weeks to implement the system, but focusing on this data made everything simpler and more practical. And the CEO said that the five numbers "gave me 85% of the information I needed to know how sales were doing."

Find *your* Special Numbers: they are the *inputs* that generate the *output* of actual sales. This is the data that really matters. When sales agents plan their selling activity around these numbers, track them while they work, and discuss them with their managers in one-to-one conversations, they transform their ability to sell. When sales managers collect these numbers on a regular basis and learn how to "read" them, they know the coaching and training required to develop their team members. Make all of this a learning experience—not an occasion for blame and making people wrong—and you'll create a sales engine that sustains itself over time.

And you'll watch sales rise dramatically.

Sales managers and CEOs often ask, "But what if the agents lie about the numbers, what if they just make stuff up?" Not to worry. The questions you ask will reveal any story-telling. That's the wonderful thing about focusing on *inputs* as well as *outputs*. In each case, tracking these numbers and reviewing them with rigor and curiosity will either give you results or reasons. When you're getting lots of reasons instead of results, *that's* what has to be addressed with training, coaching, and the sort of serious support that helps agents discover if this job is for them or not.

People can and *will* transform their sales performance when they compare what they *aimed to do* with what they *actually did.* Doing this without story-telling, excuse, or blame becomes a wake-up call that allows them to turn off their autopilot and turn on their brilliance. Do these things consistently and well, and you will build a sales force that is skilled, committed, and intensely proud of what they're doing. And you'll watch sales *really* start working.

Cordell Jacks and Tamara Baker, who built from scratch the most successful sanitation marketing project in the world, reflected recently on their experience. Cordell said, "I came from a sales background, but I never knew that the experience of building a sales force could be so open, so enjoyable, and so incredibly rewarding." Tamara added, "I expected to learn how to manage salespeople. What I didn't expect was that my entire life would be changed. I'm so proud of what we did and so very grateful for how the experience has transformed me."

Learn to *build* your salespeople and watch them change their lives for the better.

YOUR VERY NEXT STEPS

Transformation doesn't run by the clock. It makes its own time, and you can learn to follow its progress and know when to make your next move. Start simply, learn as you go, and experiment at your own pace, keeping in mind your unique enterprise, the size and shape of your sales force, and your position of influence within it.

Here are four steps our clients have found helpful to take:

1. Start with Yourself

You've probably heard Gandhi's advice on leadership: "Be the change you want to see." In the words of Bob Leitner, one of Scott's early mentors, "You can't lead where you won't go, and you can't teach what you don't know." [xxv]

> "You can't lead where you won't go, and you can't teach what you don't know."

So, over the next few days, experiment with the parts of this book that have interested you the most. Try things out. Don't expect it all to fall into place, but don't keep banging your head against the wall either. Follow your curiosity.

You might start by paying attention to your state of mind. Notice when you're Above-the-Line and when you're Below-the-Line. Don't judge yourself; just watch your attitude rise and fall.

Perhaps you're interested in exploring the experience of Split Attention. Leave yourself some reminders to spend 1-2 minutes at a time, several times a day. When you begin an activity, use the phrases "I want…" and "I want *that* because I want…" to discover the Deep Desire that underlies what you're after.

You might want to quite consciously follow the steps of a CLEAR™ conversation as you talk with colleagues and customers. Spend half your discussion *learning* what *they* think, want, or suggest. Ask for permission *before* offering your own opinions. Make sure the conversation concludes with Very Next Steps, and then take them.

Or, on a Friday, before you leave for the weekend, you might want to write an Aim Plan for the following week. Start each day of that week by focusing on what you will do to fulfill that plan and see what happens.

You'll know that you're ready for step two when you notice changes in your thoughts and behavior *and* when people closest to you notice these changes as well. That's transformation at work. *Trust* this process; doing it for yourself *equips* you to introduce it to others.

2. Watch What's Happening

Pull together the key people in your organization; share what you're doing and why you're doing it. See if they want to join you on the transformational journey. Together, *get into the field* and observe your salespeople and your sales managers as they work. Keep track of what you notice them doing and ask them for the thinking behind their activity. Resist giving advice or suggestions—just keep observing and learning.

Use the R=A+C+E™ formula to organize your observations. Clarify the results people are seeking. Notice their attitude as they work—when it's up and when it's down. Assess their competence as they interact with others—which parts of CLEAR™ they do well and which need more work. Pay close attention to *how* people sell and manage salespeople. What is the *real* selling system at work in your company, and what do people *actually* do to execute it? What is the *real* sales management structure that your managers employ, and what *actually* happens when they engage their direct reports?

> Use the R=A+C+E™ formula to organize your observations.

Make a list of the problems you need to solve to transform your sales organization. Put them in priority order. You'll know this step is complete when you have a prioritized list and a written calculation of what it is costing your company to leave these problems unsolved. Is your reputation being damaged or your mission compromised by the way you're selling? You may well find that you're paying a *qualitative* price that's even greater than the *quantitative* one. This awareness of *cost* is the foundation of your business case for change.

3. Experiment with the Best

Choose your best people—those who are high performers *and* great learners—and, together, design a pilot program in which you can develop a DQ Selling system that's right for your customers. Develop the practices and structure that will support them to make the system work. Develop a Sight Seller to keep both agent and customer on track in the sales conversation. Identify the four or five Special Numbers that focus on the input activities that generate the output of sales.

Then, try out what you've got. Hold a training in which this group can *experience* a transformed way of thinking and acting. Learn as you go, change to meet the challenges that emerge, stay the course, and measure the results—outputs *and* inputs.

You'll know this step is complete when you're getting the results you want *and* the understanding of how you got them.

4. Roll It Out to the Rest

When you've got a selling system that works—one that produces sales results *and* increased well-being for everyone involved— figure out how to roll it out to the rest of your sales force, starting with the people who are *most ready and able to change.*

One word of caution: Not everyone will welcome this activity with open arms. That's a *good* thing. Your program becomes a line in the sand—declaring what it takes to sell and to manage sales in *your* company. Within a month or two, you'll find that about half your sales force is really catching on, most of the rest are giving it a go but struggling with parts of the process, and a small percentage are opting out—quitting the process or quitting the company.

You'll know it's working when your sales force is committing instead of hedging, getting great instead of getting by, and staying on track instead of just staying busy. And the sales results will speak for themselves.

It's a great adventure. Go, make it happen.

THANK YOU

We'd be delighted to hear from you. Share with us your stories, your feedback, or any other conversation that supports the sales transformation you want to lead.

You can reach us through our website, **WRPartnership.com,** or by writing us directly at: **connect@WRPartnership.com.**

—Roy and Scott

OUR INTERVIEWS

We have been privileged to work with many wonderful clients and partners over the years. We interviewed 21 of them for this book. We thank them for their generosity, inspiration, and vision for a world that works for everyone. We urge you to visit their websites and support their work.

Esther Altorfer is the East Africa Managing Director of **Sistema. bio**, which provides farmers with high-efficiency biodigesters that take organic waste and transform it into renewal biogas and a powerful organic fertilizer. Visit: https://Sistema.bio.

Maggie Appleton is the COO of **Educate!**, which tackles youth unemployment by partnering with youth, schools, and governments to design and deliver education solutions that equip young people in Africa with the skills to attain further education, overcome gender inequities, start businesses, get jobs, and drive development in their communities. Visit: www.ExperienceEducate.org.

Tamara Baker and Cordell Jacks worked with Mike Roberts of **iDE Cambodia** to create the Sanitation Marketing Scale-Up program (SMSU). They trained and supported entrepreneurs who manufactured, sold, and installed latrines in rural Cambodia. It became the largest program of its kind in the world. See the report: https://s3.amazonaws.com/www.ideglobal.org/files/public/SMSU_Learning_Report_FINAL_5.22.2019.pdf?mtime=20190724150932.

Eduardo Bontempo is Co-Founder of **Geekie**, a São Paulo-based educational technology company that provides a range of web and mobile applications that integrate with school curriculums to guide teachers in their work. Visit: www.Geekie.com.br.

Gayatri Datar is the Co-Founder and CEO of **EarthEnable**, which turns earthen-floor homes into affordable, sanitary flooring that can be washed, cleaned, and used to create a healthy home environment. Visit: www.EarthEnable.org.

Lizz Ellis, CEO of **iDE**, leads a global team of 1,175 changemakers with the belief that one entrepreneur can change their community and millions can change the world. iDE was founded by Paul Polak in 1982 and, to date, has lifted over 35 million people out of poverty. Visit www.iDEGlobal.org. For more on Lizz Ellis, please see: https://www.iDEGlobal.org/people/elizabeth-ellis-ceo.

Karen Genzink was one of the earliest consultants at **Whitten & Roy Partnership**. Over the seven years she worked with us, she sold, designed, and delivered multiple projects in Africa, Asia, and Mexico.

Laura Hattendorf is the Head of Grants and Investments at the **Mulago Foundation** and a Lecturer at the **Stanford Graduate School of Business**, where she teaches a course for aspiring impact entrepreneurs. Visit: www.MulagoFoundation.org and https://www.GSB.Stanford.edu/faculty-research/faculty/laura-hattendorf.

Klann Mab is currently the National Operations Manager for **iDE Cambodia**'s Sanitation Marketing Scale-Up program (SMSU). They are working to defeat diarrheal disease by selling latrines and water filters to the rural poor. Visit: www.iDE-Global.org/country/cambodia.

Erica Mackey and Beth Szymanski are the Co-Founders of **MyVillage** They empower stay-at-home parents and anyone looking for a career change to start their own childcare or preschool program and make a big difference in little lives. Visit: www.MyVillage.com.

Kola Masha is the Managing Director of **Babban Gona**, which works with smallholder farmers to make more money by providing inputs on credit, modern agricultural methods, and market access to sell their harvests. Visit: www.BabbanGona.com.

Lisa Mikkelsen is Head of Global Human Capital at **Flourish Ventures** (a spin-out of the Omidyar Network). They are a venture firm investing in entrepreneurs whose innovations help people achieve financial health and prosperity. Visit: https://FlourishVentures.com.

Anushka Ratnayake is the Founder and CEO of **myAgro**. They move farmers out of poverty by providing planting advice and a mobile layaway program to finance their purchase of agricultural supplies. Visit: www.myAgro.org.

Mike Roberts is the Country Director of **iDE Cambodia**. They have been growing prosperity in Cambodia since 1984 by building value chains and business models in agriculture, clean water, and sanitation that promote beneficial, affordable products and services. Visit: www.iDEGlobal.org/country/cambodia.

Chhavi Sharma is the International Programme Manager at **Ashden**. Through an integrated program of awards, business support, and connections to finance, they create an ecosystem of support for entrepreneurs in the UK and around the world who are accelerating transformative climate solutions. Visit: www.Ashden.org.

Kevin Starr leads the **Mulago Foundation**. They find and fund high-performance organizations that tackle the basic needs of the very poor and have a high potential for scale. Visit: www.MulagoFoundation.org.

John Stone is the Founder and Chairman of the **Stone Family Foundation**, They bring a business-like approach to helping people out of poverty, and they focus on market-based solutions to problems of water and sanitation in the developing world. Visit: www.theSFF.com.

Lindsay Stradley is the Co-Founder of **Sanergy**. They design, build, and deliver sanitation products and services that are an effective alternative to sewers in today's growing cities. In one of their operational areas, Nairobi's urban slums, they have built a network of over 3,000 sanitation units offering an affordable, clean, and safe sanitation experience to the residents. Visit: www.Sanergy.com.

Jim Taylor is the Co-Founder and CEO of **Proximity Designs**. They are a social enterprise in Myanmar that designs and delivers affordable, income-boosting products that complement the entrepreneurial spirit of rural families. Visit: www. ProximityDesigns.org.

ACKNOWLEDGMENTS

This book is a product of the working relationship we've enjoyed over the past 35 years. That relationship has been influenced and informed by many teachers, mentors, colleagues, and friends.

You know who you are, and we trust that you know the gratitude we feel for your contribution to our lives. We wouldn't be doing this and doing it in this way if it weren't for you.

With the certainty that we're leaving somebody out, and with our apologies for doing so, we recognize the following people who have especially contributed to the thinking and practices that have shaped this book: our fellow consultants at WRP; our customers, many of whom have become friends; Nicole and her talented team at Niche Pressworks; and a special word of gratitude to our own COO, Jessica Gustafson, for her editorial expertise.

We especially acknowledge our many clients and partners in the world of social enterprises. The privilege of working with you has given our work its deepest meaning.

And, as always, we thank our families for creating a centered and strong "home" from which we can depart to do our work and to which we can return to be replenished.

ABOUT THE AUTHORS

W. Roy Whitten and Scott A. Roy are the co-founders of the international sales consultancy, Whitten & Roy Partnership. WRP maintains a global consultant network and has guided businesses and organizations in over 40 countries to transform the way they sell.

Roy Whitten is an expert in transformative learning and its role in sales performance. In 2004, he earned a PhD for his work in transformative learning and change. In over 40 years as a trainer, consultant, and coach, he has personally supported the development of thousands of people through-out the world.

Scott Roy spent the first part of his career building and running large, direct-sales organizations. He co-founded a national insurance company that has grown to over $2B in assets. Since

2005, he has been a consultant and coach to companies through-out the world.

If you'd like more information about the authors or WRP's services, please visit their website: WRPartnership.com.

ENDNOTES

i For example: David Bornstein, *How to Change the World: Social Entrepreneurs and the Power of New Ideas* (Oxford University Press, Inc., 2007); Paul Polak, *Out of Poverty: What Works When Traditional Approaches Fail* (Barret-Koehler Publishers, Inc., 2008); and Mohammad Yunus, *Creating a World Without Poverty: Social Business and the Future of Capitalism* (PublicAffairs, 2007).

ii Polak, *Out of Poverty*, Introduction.

iii See their website: https://www.millersocent.org/about/.

iv See the work of Jack Mezirow. Or look at the curriculum for transformative studies at places like the California Institute of Integral Studies, where Roy received his PhD in 2004.

v   This parable is attributed to G.I. Gurdjieff by authors
        P.D. Ouspensky, Charles T. Tart, and Jacob Needleman.

vi   Jeffrey M. Schwartz, M.D., and Sharon Begley, *The
        Mind and the Brain: Neuroplasticity and the Power of
        Mental Force* (New York: Harper Collins ebooks). Also,
        see the work of cognitive researchers and therapists
        Albert Ellis and Aaron T. Beck.

vii   See the work of neuroscientist Joseph E. LeDoux.

viii   Oxford English Dictionary.

ix   David Eagleman, Incognito: The Secret Lives of the
        Brain (New York: First Vintage Books, 2011).

x   Proverb, often attributed to Idris Shah, the Sufi author
        and teacher.

xi   Lewis Carroll, Alice's Adventures in Wonderland (New
        York: Millennium Publications), chapter VI.

xii   If you want help with this, we recommend the best
        book we've found on the subject: David Allen, Getting
        Things Done: The Art of Stress-Free Productivity (New
        York: Viking Penguin, 2001).

xiii   Maxwell Maltz, Psycho-Cybernetics: A New Way
        to Get More Living Out of Life (New York: Simon &
        Schuster, 1960).

xiv   The esoteric Russian philosopher, Gurdjieff, as
        recounted by his colleague, P.D. Ouspensky, In
        Search of the Miraculous (New York: Harcourt Brace
        Jovanovich, 1949), 14-15.

xv   We acknowledge Dr. John Hoover who created this
        approach and has licensed our use of it.

xvi Charles T. Tart, Waking Up: Overcoming the Obstacles to Human Potential (New Science Library, Shambala, 1987), ix.

xvii John Moyne and Coleman Barks, Open Secret: Versions of Rumi (Shambala, 1999).

xviii When he approved for publication what we included from his interview, Mab added: "Learning to manage my attitude has had a positive impact on my work. It has taken me to the next level of selling. I'm very proud to have played a part in impacting Cambodia through our sanitation program. We have sold 377,059 toilets to date!"

xix We gratefully acknowledge the pioneering work of our colleague and friend, Dr. John Hoover, who licensed us to incorporate his mapping of below-the-line attitudes into this model.

xx W. Roy Whitten, "Awake and Aware: the Practice of Split Attention in Everyday Life" (PhD diss., California Institute of Integral Studies, San Francisco, 2004). Split Attention is a variation of what Gurdjieff called self-remembrance and Ouspensky called divided attention.

xxi Schwartz and Begley.

xxii We acknowledge David Allen for this concept, and, again, we recommend his book, Getting Things Done, for anyone looking for guidance about handling their information flow, developing their priorities, and handling how to move their projects forward.

xxiii   Zig Ziglar.

xxiv   Mihaly Csikszentmihalyi, *Flow: The Psychology of Optimal Experience* (New York: Harper Perennial, 1990).

xxv   Bob Lightener, one of Scott's early mentors.

ALSO FROM ROY WHITTEN AND SCOTT ROY...

Sell Well, Do Good shows you how to transform your business-to-consumer (B2C) sales. If you also engage in business-to-business (B2B) selling—if you wholesale your goods and services, if you deal with governments or NGOs, if you seek support from investors—you many find *Decision Intelligence Selling* to be of significant help.

Visit www.wrpartnership.com for more information, supportive downloads, and purchasing links.

Lightning Source UK Ltd.
Milton Keynes UK
UKHW022039090621
385225UK00001B/12/J